A Practical Guide to Compe
How to enhance individual and c
performance

Steve Whiddett
Sarah Hollyforde

Steve Whiddett BSc (Hons), MSc, C.Psychol, is a chartered occupational psychologist. He has over 25 years' experience as a specialist in the areas of assessment and development. Steve has presented at conferences and published many articles on these topics. steve@whe-uk.com

Sarah Hollyforde MCIPD, MBA, is a professionally qualified human resources (HR) manager. She has over 20 years' experience in both the private and public sector. Sarah draws on her experiences in implementing and sur̄ ̄s. sarah@whe-uk.com

Whether you are encountering competencies for the first time, or indeed have some or little experience of their application in the workplace, this updated version of The Competencies Handbook is able to guide you through all the intricacies in a simple easy to understand format.

As the authors themselves comment 'competencies typically form the foundations of core HR processes', therefore this is an idea HR reference book which can be used by all levels of HR practitioners as they go about their daily duties. It will help them to add value to any debate with line management in respect of the world of competencies.

John Gloak
HR Director, IT and Operations, Lloyds TSB Bank plc

The book is a great read in its entirety, but is also well structured for use as a reference guide. The use of real world examples is very effective. As the director of a small, relatively new company, I see the book as being a valuable tool to assist us, and similar organisations, in the development of a new competency framework. Equally, for those organisations that already have well-developed competency frameworks, the book will help ensure they are making best use of them, for example in the areas of recruitment and training and development. I'm sure readers will find references to the potential pitfalls and the identification of 'what not do' invaluable.

Andrew Stephens
Director, Local Government Data Unit, Wales

Competencies have become ubiquitous. They are part of every solution to any people-related problem. They are so prevalent that they are almost being taken for granted. There is a certain degree of complacency that has developed as a result. Very different organisations have very similar competency frameworks? Why? How? Too many organisations have too many competencies. How can these be reliably used? How effective are they?

This book is a very useful antidote to that complacency. It provides a valuable and comprehensive overview of the whole competency field. It provides the theoretical background to competencies, which is important to appreciate if they are to be properly understood, as well as providing highly practical information about identifying and implementing competencies. This book provides everything you need to know about competencies.

Rajvinder Kandola
Founding Partner, Pearn Kandola

The Chartered Institute of Personnel and Development is the leading publisher of books and reports for personnel and training professionals, students, and all those concerned with the effective management and development of people at work. For details of all our titles, please contact the publishing department:
tel: 020–8263 3387
fax: 020–8263 3850
email publish@cipd.co.uk
The catalogue of all CIPD titles can be viewed on the CIPD website:
www.cipd.co.uk/bookstore

A Practical Guide to Competencies:
How to enhance individual and organisational performance

Steve Whiddett

Sarah Hollyforde

Chartered Institute of Personnel and Development

Published by the Chartered Institute of Personnel and Development, CIPD House,
Camp Road, London, SW19 4UX

First published as The Competencies Handbook 1999

Design and typeset by Fakenham Photosetting, Fakenham, Norfolk
Printed in Great Britain by The Cromwell Press, Trowbridge, Wiltshire

British Library Cataloguing in Publication Data
A catalogue of this publication is available from the British Library

ISBN 1 84398 012 6

The views expressed in this publication are the author's own and may not necessarily
reflect those of the CIPD.

The CIPD has made every effort to trace and acknowledge copyright holders. If any
source has been overlooked, CIPD Enterprises would be pleased to redress this for
future editions.

Chartered Institute of Personnel and Development, CIPD House,
Camp Road, London, SW19 4UX
Tel: 020 8971 9000   Fax: 020 8263 3333
E-mail: cipd@cipd.co.uk   Website: www.cipd.co.uk
Incorporated by Royal Charter.   Registered Charity No. 1079797

Acknowledgements

We would like to thank again all those people who helped us with the first edition of this book. We would also like to thank our teachers, colleagues and clients, in numerous organisations, who have helped shape and develop the knowledge, experience and expertise that we have drawn on in producing this second edition of *A Practical Guide to Competencies* (formerly *The Competencies Handbook*.)

Contents

List of Figures

List of tables

Introduction

Since we wrote the first edition of this handbook, competencies have continued to increase in popularity. While the phrase 'people are our key asset' has been overused to the point that it can sound rather empty, organisations are increasingly realising that they are no longer able to rely entirely on a good product to give them a competitive edge. The contribution that people make to *how* a job gets done, and thereby the service customers receive, is becoming key to giving companies a good (or poor!) reputation.

It was recently reported (*Competency & Emotional Intelligence Journal*, 2002/03) that some organisations are taking the contribution of their people seriously enough to measure their 'key assets' in the same way they measure assets such as capital, profits and equipment. Much of this measurement is based around competencies because competency frameworks provide a link between business objectives and people-management policies and practices.

Competencies now feature in many people-management policies and practices. In some organisations competency frameworks are used in one or two applications; in others they form the central focus of all human resource (HR) activities. However, while a potentially powerful tool to help manage the performance of people at work, competencies are not a panacea for people management issues in organisations.

Organisations' experiences with competencies have been many and varied. Many organisations have developed excellent competency frameworks and implemented these with great effect. Some organisations have had bad experiences trying to design and develop competencies, leading to even worse experiences when trying to implement them and trying to make them work – so much so that some organisations refuse to use the term 'competencies', even though that is what they are using. In almost all cases, these bad experiences could have been avoided with appropriate guidance and a better understanding of what competencies are and what they can and cannot do.

Competencies need to be well-designed and well-developed. To be implemented effectively they need to be built into well-designed people-management processes. And, as we asserted in the first edition, recent research (*Competency & Emotional Intelligence Journal*, 2002) confirms that the intended users of a competency framework need to be involved in its development to encourage ownership and acceptance of it as a valid tool. In addition, users need appropriate skills to use these processes and they need to understand how competencies contribute alongside other performance criteria to help make the process effective.

THE ROLE OF COMPETENCY FRAMEWORKS

Performance criteria have been used in the past to define the required standards for a job applicant. Similarly, performance criteria have been used to monitor and manage job performance through appraisals, and training and development programmes have been designed and evaluated using performance criteria.

As human-resources (HR) departments have become more integrated it makes sense to have one common set of criteria to cover common themes in different people-management processes. This would ensure that key criteria used to select an individual are also used to monitor and manage their performance and to focus their training and development. Competencies are an efficient way of providing a common framework of performance criteria for use across the full range of people-management processes.

A common framework of performance criteria for all people-management processes has two further benefits, as it provides:

■ a common language across all parts of an organisation for describing effectiveness in that organisation. For example, users of the framework will have a common understanding of what good leadership looks like or what it means to be effective when working in a team

■ an opportunity to achieve a high level of consistency when assessing performance. Whether for selection or in appraisal, all 'assessors' will know what good performance should look like and will know what needs to be assessed and what can be ignored.

Where a competency framework covers a range of job levels – eg supervisors through to senior managers – it also provides individuals with the opportunity to identify and plan their competency development in order to pursue progression to other roles.

As mentioned earlier, competencies can help organisations to integrate HR applications. Successful organisations have been those that have used competencies as tools within these applications. They have also been clear about the potential limitations of competencies and what they cannot do. Organisations need to keep competencies in their rightful place – in the background of the application. It is the application that is important: competencies just help to make the application effective.

Competencies typically form the foundations of core HR processes. The following applications remain the most popular and each has a chapter dedicated to it in this book.

■ selection and assessment
■ reviewing performance and appraisal
■ training and development
■ pay and grading.

Competencies provide a common set of criteria in the form of behavioural indicators. However, each of these processes requires more than one set of criteria to be fully effective. For example:

■ Selection will usually take account of a person's experience, past performance and job-relevant qualifications.
■ Training takes account of job tasks and what needs to be achieved.
■ Development takes account of organisational and individual needs.
■ Reward is based on job worth as well as the need to reward and motivate individual performance.

The introduction of competencies can increase consistency between these applications. However, the introduction of competencies cannot alone guarantee that these applications will be more effective. The most comprehensive competency framework, no matter how well-designed and appropriate, will not make a bad process good, nor will it compensate for poor training, poor techniques or unskilled users. However, where effective and appropriate processes are allied with appropriate tools and skilled users, competencies can help significantly to improve the standards and consistency of people-management processes and performance within an organisation.

WHAT IS IN THIS BOOK?

The increase in the use of competencies means that there are different views about the definition, applications and structure of competencies and competency frameworks. We explore the origins of 'competencies', discuss various definitions of competencies and what we mean by 'competency' in Chapter 1. In Chapter 2 we describe the structure of a typical competency framework and the quality standards that a good competency framework should match up to. Chapter 3 describes the key stages for producing or adapting competency frameworks, the issues that have to be considered when designing a good competency framework and key principles which underpin competency framework development. Each of the subsequent four chapters is devoted to one of the four most popular applications and discusses the factors that affect that application and how competencies can contribute.

In each of the applications chapters we investigate:

- the purpose of that application
- the factors that influence the application
- the contribution that competencies can make.

Three appendices are provided. Appendix 1 provides a sample competency framework that is used to illustrate points made throughout the book. This is referred to throughout the book as the **Appendix Framework**. Appendix 2 provides a checklist for comparing elements of competency frameworks with the qualities required of a good competency framework. Appendix 3 outlines a process for producing competency-based role profiles.

HOW SHOULD THIS BOOK BE USED?

All readers should read the first two chapters in the order they are presented in the book. The chapter on producing and adapting a competency framework and the four applications chapters have been written in such a way that they can be read in any order or read selectively, depending on the reader's objectives or interests.

WHO IS THE BOOK AIMED AT?

We have written this guide for anyone with an interest in the management of people and/or with an involvement in the introduction or maintenance of a competency framework in their organisation. Anyone introducing new people-management processes within an organisation is also likely to find this book extremely helpful. We have focused most on readers who have an understanding of people-management processes and who may want to know more about how competencies could be used within them.

This book is not a training manual. If you are uncertain about the specific techniques and skills required to design and/or implement competencies, seek appropriate advice and use this book to help you ensure that your adviser is competent, experienced and well-informed.

It has been our intention, in this book, to share our knowledge and experience in order to enhance the reader's knowledge and help them develop their people-management practices. If you need further information then please ask us – we are always happy to answer queries from our readers.

REFERENCES AND READING

RANKIN N. (2002) 'Benchmarking Survey'. *Competency & Emotional Intelligence*. (Benchmarking edition). pp2–22.

SCARBROUGH H. and ELIAS J. (2002/03) 'Evaluating Human Capital'. As reported in 'Competency-based software paves the way for human capital approach'. *Competency & Emotional Intelligence*. Vol. 10, No.2, Winter. p2.

What do we mean by 'competencies'?

CHAPTER 1

Competencies are about capability – the things that individuals or organisations are and/or need to be good at. We briefly touch on organisational competency later in this chapter but our focus is on the competency of individuals. This book is about competencies used as performance criteria: the performance standards expected of people capable of contributing positively to organisational performance.

Not surprisingly, perhaps, people with different interests look at competency in different ways. Some people are interested in the extent to which individuals are competent at completing the detailed tasks and activities that make up their jobs. Some people are more interested in the way in which competent people behave when working. Others make little or no distinction between the tasks people undertake and how people behave. Consequently, competencies mean different things to different people. To avoid confusion this chapter looks at different views of competency and provides the definition of competency that is used throughout the remainder of this book.

DEFINITIONS OF COMPETENCY

Difficulties in implementing competencies often arise from a lack of understanding or lack of agreement about what a competency is. The number of definitions of competency continues to grow. However, most definitions are variations on two well-established themes from different origins.

Main themes

The two main themes in the definition of competencies are:

- *Descriptions of work tasks* ie what a person has to do in a job. These have their origins in national training schemes, such as the National/Scottish Vocational Qualifications and the Management Charter Initiative (MCI)
- *Descriptions of behaviour* ie how a person does their job. These have evolved from the work of researchers and consultants specialising in managerial effectiveness.

A general convention has developed, although it is not always followed, which uses 'competence' or 'competency', depending upon what is being described:

- An ability based on work tasks is usually referred to as a '*competence*' (plural competences) – *what* they have to achieve.
- An ability based on behaviour is usually referred to as a '*competency*' (plural competencies) – *how* they have to achieve.

Table 1 (overleaf) illustrates the differences between the two definitions.

Table 1 *Key differences between competency and competence*

	Competency	**Competence**
Focus	*The person*	*The job/role*
Summary of	*Behaviours observed in effective people*	*Related tasks in the job/roles*
Examples	Interpersonal effectiveness	Dealing with enquiries
Performance indicators	*Behavioural statements*	*Outputs from the job, task or role*
Examples	Adapts style of interaction to take account of feelings of others	Accurately completes enquiry forms
		Replies within agreed deadlines
	Shares information to gain commitment from others	Accurately enters details on database

In practice, some organisations include tasks, outputs and behaviours in their competence/competency frameworks and some even blend them together. Unless task-based competences and behaviour-based competencies are kept separate the result can be very confusing. We advise keeping them separate.

Competences are usually job- or role-specific while *competencies* can cover a wide range of different jobs and often cover different levels of job as well. This ability of competencies to cover a wide range of jobs has contributed significantly to their popularity. This book focuses on developing and using competencies (sets of which are collectively referred to as competency frameworks).

Just as there are different views about competence and competency, there are also various definitions of competency – usually based on the following:

a job competency is 'an underlying characteristic of a person which results in effective and/or superior performance in a job' (Klemp, 1980).

Variations typically expand on what the characteristics may be – as, for example, in this much-quoted definition:

'A job competency is an underlying characteristic of a person in that it may be a motive, a trait, a skill, an aspect of one's self-image or social role, or a body of knowledge which he or she uses' (Boyatzis, 1982).

Competencies do not simply list characteristics such as motives, traits or skills – eg 'able to communicate clearly' or 'prefers rewards to be based on results' or 'has good hand-eye co-ordination'. Competencies provide examples of what we would see when people use these characteristics effectively. For example, communicating clearly and preferring rewards to be based on results might contribute to several different behaviours when observing an effective salesperson. Competencies help to assess how people combine and use knowledge, abilities, motives, etc when tackling job tasks, rather than simply measuring knowledge, abilities or motives in isolation.

INFLUENCES ON COMPETENCY

In addition to the characteristics of the individual and the demands of their specific job tasks, there are other influences on competency. These other influences might be described as the context within which the individual works. Many organisations have attempted to define this context in terms of a mission statement, a company vision and/or a set of principles or values. Given that the organisational context provides parameters for the behaviour of the individual, any definition of competency needs to take this into account. All behaviours within a competency framework should be consistent with the organisational context, ie its values, mission, vision, culture, etc.

Adding value

A company had a set of values that included 'Pioneering – seeking to be at the forefront of current thinking'. They ensured that the behaviours in their competency framework, where appropriate, reflected this value. For example, under the competency 'Business Focus', one of the behaviours was 'Keeps up to date with current thinking in the sector', and in the competency 'Customer Service', one of the behaviours was 'Uses knowledge of customers' needs to develop new products and services'.

By linking competencies to its mission and values, an organisation is not only clearly stating their commitment to the values, but also integrating the behaviours that support them throughout the management of people.

Our definition of competencies

The definition of competencies used in this book is based on behaviour observed within the organisation setting:

 'competencies are behaviours that individuals demonstrate when undertaking job-relevant tasks effectively within a given organisational context'.

In the following example (taken from the **Appendix Framework**), note that context is explicit in the level definitions and further contextual information is included in the bullet-point examples.

MANAGING PERFORMANCE: Inspires ownership and achievement of standards

Level 1 *Ensures performance management is effective across the business*
- balances the management of people and initiatives across the business
- takes account of the needs of own and others' departments when setting objectives
- uses best-practice benchmarks to monitor performance of departments.

Level 2 *Provides effective management support for their department*
- effectively balances management of people, tasks and activities
- encourages others to have a realistic view of their career prospects
- takes account of the needs of team members when agreeing objectives.

Level 3 *Manages day-to-day performance constructively, fairly and promptly*
- openly recognises and rewards good performance
- acts quickly and fairly to address poor performance
- demonstrates the importance of performance management by giving it a high priority
- is open to and encourages feedback from all levels in the business
- visibly and quickly deals with those who harass, bully or unfairly discriminate.

OTHER TYPES OF COMPETENCY

Although we have covered the two main themes of competency, there are two other types of competency that readers may have heard of – organisational competences and meta-competencies.

Organisational competences

Organisational competences are the things that organisations are best at. For example, Prahalad and Hamel (1990) suggested that 3M had core competence in sticky tape and Honda in engines. As can be seen from the descriptions, these are not behavioural competencies, but technical, know-how-type competences. We will not be discussing them further in this book.

Meta-competencies

When recruiting and developing high-fliers in junior roles for future senior management positions, organisations can't be sure what competencies will be required so far in the future. Factors that distinguish high-fliers now for roles in perhaps 10 years' time are therefore broader than those used to select or develop people for current or short-term future roles.

Kandola and Galpin (2002) outlined 11 meta-competencies that could be used alongside current competency frameworks to assess people for long-term development into senior roles. These include:

- seeks opportunities to learn
- adapts to cultural differences
- brings out the best in people.

We touch on these again in Chapter 6 (**Using Competencies for Training and Development**).

COMPETENCY FRAMEWORKS AND EMOTIONAL INTELLIGENCE

Emotional Intelligence (EQ), first made popular through the writings of Daniel Goleman, is based on the idea that the more aware people are of their own emotions, and the emotions of others, the more emotionally intelligent they are. Within the work context, EQ will inform a person's ability to be self-motivated, manage a team effectively, cope effectively with pressure and so on.

EQ in relation to its application at work is still relatively new. It is not surprising, therefore, that there is still much confusion about the subject. One leading researcher into EQ feels that 'many programmes that are labelled "emotional intelligence" have little to do with either emotions or intelligence, but, instead, are simply repackaged competency, development or assessment programmes' (Caruso, 2001).

There clearly is a link between EQ and competencies, and a good generic framework will contain behaviours based on EQ concepts, thus making a specific EQ-based framework unnecessary.

In this book we do not make specific mention of EQ competencies. Examples of EQ will be incorporated into competencies, where appropriate, through the use of a thorough competency framework design process, as outlined in the following chapters.

KEY POINTS

- There are many types and definitions of competency.
- Competences are based on job tasks and are job-specific.
- Competencies are based on behavioural statements and can cover many jobs.
- Competencies describe what we see when people use underlying characteristics, eg knowledge, abilities and motives, to tackle job-relevant tasks.
- The definition of competency used in this book is 'Competencies are behaviours that effective individuals demonstrate when undertaking job-relevant tasks within a given organisational context.'
- Meta-competencies help identify people with potential for long-term development.
- Organisational competences describe the core capability of organisations.
- Emotional Intelligence behaviours will be represented in well-defined and comprehensive competency frameworks.

REFERENCES AND READING

BOYATZIS R. E. (1982) *The Competent Manager: A model for effective performance.* Chichester, John Wiley & Sons.

CARUSO D. (2001) 'Emotionally intelligent working'. *Competency & Emotional Intelligence.* Vol. 9, No. 1, Autumn 2001. p26.

KANDOLA R. and GALPIN M. (2002) 'Assessing and developing high-fliers: the case for meta-competencies'. *Competency & Emotional Intelligence.* Vol. 10, No. 2, Winter 2002/03. pp20–24.

KLEMP G. O. Jnr (1980) *The Assessment of Occupational Competence.* Report to the National Institute of Education, Washington, DC.

PRAHALAD C.K. and HAMEL G. (1990) 'The core competence of the organisation'. *Harvard Business Review.* Vol. 68, May–June 1990. pp57–69.

A typical competency framework

There can be a lot of detail within a competency framework. This detail needs to be accessed quickly and easily if users are to consider the framework to be a worthwhile tool. Competencies therefore need to be organised in some structured way to aid their use.

As with any tool, cheap ones made with poor materials might look good, but do not last long. Carefully designed tools constructed from good materials last much longer and will develop a reputation for their usefulness and for their manufacturers.

In this chapter we explore a typical, good competency framework: what it will look like and its qualities.

TYPICAL COMPETENCY FRAMEWORK STRUCTURES

Competency framework structures vary from organisation to organisation, although many contain similar features and similar competencies. Some organisations take an existing framework and adapt it for their own use; many start from scratch. The question of whether a competency framework should be 'off-the-shelf' or 'bespoke' is addressed in Chapter 3 (**Developing Competency Frameworks**). Despite the various approaches to constructing competency frameworks, they have the same basic elements and are often organised in a similar way.

A common structure for a basic framework is depicted in Figure 1.

In the structure shown in Figure 1, behavioural indicators (example behaviours) are the basic elements or building-blocks. Related behavioural indicators are organised into competencies, either as a straightforward list or within a number of different levels. Related competencies are then organised into

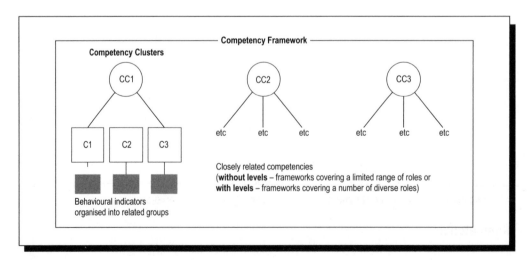

Figure 1 *A typical competency framework structure*

competency clusters. Each of these elements is described below, starting with the basic building-blocks – ie the behavioural indicators.

Behavioural indicators

Let's start with a reminder of our definition of competencies:

 Competencies are behaviours that individuals demonstrate when undertaking job-relevant tasks effectively within a given organisational context.

Behavioural indicators are examples of the behaviours, from our definition of competencies, that would be observed when someone demonstrates competency.

In most cases, behavioural indicators are examples of effective competency. Examples of poor or ineffective competency, often referred to as contra-indicators, may also be observed and are included in some frameworks, eg 'uses time and other resources inefficiently'. In our experience, contra-indicators are often opposites of positive behaviours and can be avoided.

In our **Appendix Framework** (see page 132) all of the behavioural indicators are examples of effective competency. For example, behavioural indicators for 'SHOWS THE WAY: Direction, Level 3 ' are:

- focuses and encourages others to focus on delivering the business goals
- regularly reviews and communicates progress on business goals
- uses the business goals to prioritise work.

It is not necessary, or indeed possible, to provide examples of all behaviours that could be observed within a competency. The behaviours that are included normally indicate the type of behaviour that is expected to be observed – hence 'behavioural indicators'. In many frameworks, the behavioural indicators will relate to several jobs and, when using the competency framework, the indicators may need to be added to and made relevant to specific jobs. For example, the **Appendix Framework** (see page 133) has a competency called 'Planning' in the SHOWS THE WAY cluster. One of the behaviours in Planning: Level 3 is:

- sets SMART objectives for self and/or team

This is a generic statement. If, for example, a sales manager's performance was being reviewed using this competency, job-specific examples of the behaviour would be used. For example:

- agrees SMART objectives with their manager for own sales and sales team, in line with departmental objectives
- sets SMART objectives with each sales team member in line with departmental objectives.

How to adapt generic indicators for specific applications is covered in more detail in Chapter 3 (**Developing a Competency Framework**) and the relevant practical chapters.

Competencies

Each competency is a collection of related behavioural indicators. For example, behaviours relating to teamworking will be grouped together in a competency with a 'teamworking' theme and behaviours relating to getting things done will be grouped together in a competency with an 'achieving results' theme and so on. In the simplest frameworks there will be one list of behavioural indicators for each competency. Frameworks covering several levels of jobs may have several lists or levels of behavioural indicators per competency.

Competencies without levels

A simple framework – eg one that covers large numbers of jobs that place very similar behavioural demands on their jobholders – may have a single list of indicators within each competency. In this type of framework all behavioural indicators would relate to all jobs. For example, a framework which covers only senior management jobs in one organisation may include the following behavioural indicators to describe 'Planning and organising':

- produces plans which distinguish between immediate and long-term priorities (eg weeks to three years)
- produces plans which specify clear departmental objectives
- co-ordinates activities of the department in line with business plans.

A single list is all that is required, because all the behavioural indicators apply to all the senior management jobs.

Competencies with levels

When a framework covers a wide range of jobs with different demands, the behavioural indicators within each competency may be divided into separate lists or 'levels' to reflect the different degrees of demands. This is both acceptable and necessary if the competency framework is to cover a wide range of jobs or roles.

Level headers

A telecommunications company has four levels of performance for each of their competencies. For example, under their competency 'Initiating action', they have the following levels:

- acts promptly
- looks ahead and acts now
- anticipates the future and acts in difficult situations
- acts for the long term and manages risk.

In this example 'Initiating action' may be needed in both administrative and management roles. The 'initiating action' behaviours will be different for these roles, and levelling enables separate lists of behaviours to account for this in the same competency, avoiding the need for a separate framework for each role.

Most frameworks with levels distinguish between one level and another through some sort of label (eg numerically), sometimes with a brief definition. Usually, the more complex the behaviours, the higher the level. In this example from the **Appendix Framework** (see pages 132–3), levels are given a number and a definition. Note that level one is the highest level and level three is the lowest level – this enables the framework to be extended at a later date to cover non-managerial jobs without having to change all the level numbers.

PLANNING: Sets and agrees plans for self and/or others based on business goals

Level 1 ensures business plans are achievable and integrated with business goals

Level 2 ensures plans meet local needs and that they account for the needs of other teams

Level 3 uses appropriate planning to succeed in own role

Depending upon the approach used for levelling, some competencies may have only one or two levels, whereas other competencies may have several levels. For example, our **Appendix Framework** (see pages 132ff) contains two or three levels for each competency. Most contain three levels, such as 'SHOWS THE WAY: Planning' (see pages 132–3), but 'SHOWS THE WAY: Leadership' (page 132) and 'GROWS BUSINESS CAPABILITY: Customer focus' (page 134) contain only two levels each:

LEADERSHIP: Provides clear leadership consistent with our vision, mission and values

Level 1 is consistent in expectations of others and provides clear leadership

Level 2 operates openly, is accessible and approachable to others

CUSTOMER FOCUS: Uses understanding of the needs of customers to drive action

Level 1 champions customer focus throughout the business

Level 2 actively manages worthwhile relationships with customers

Some organisations relate levels directly to job grades. For example, in some frameworks all Level 1 competencies are tied to particular job grades, all Level 2 competencies are tied to the next band of job grades, and so on. This is counter-productive for two reasons. Firstly, although there is usually some connection between levels and the seniority of a job, it is not always so. For example, a senior management position may not require the job-holder to have the highest level of competency for 'managing relationships', whereas a more junior complaints-handling or account-management role may. This approach therefore restricts the number of job profiles that can be produced from the framework, as only one profile can be produced for each level of job grade.

The second way in which linking levels directly with grades is counter-productive is that a lot of time can be spent trying to create different behavioural statements for each level when, in reality, some behaviours actually overlap.

In our opinion, organisations should avoid using grade structures to dictate competency levels. Our preferred method of levelling is to group behavioural indicators by complexity of job demands as this is more much practical. Using this approach the **Appendix Framework** (see page 132) – which contains only eight competencies and a maximum of three levels per competency – could be used to produce almost 3,000 different job profiles, with small but important differences between jobs within the same grades, for example:

Job profile one

	Competency							
	1	2	3	4	5	6	7	8
Level 1							■	
Level 2		■	■			■	■	
Level 3	■	■	■	■	■	■	■	■

Job profile two

	Competency							
	1	2	3	4	5	6	7	8
Level 1								
Level 2		■	■			■		■
Level 3	■	■	■	■	■	■	■	■

Another fairly common method of levelling is to use degrees of expected performance for a job-holder. For example, a framework may include a list of behavioural indicators for each of the following:

- threshold competency – usually a minimum requirement to perform the job effectively
- outstanding competency – usually an expected level of performance for an experienced job-holder
- negative demonstrations of competency – usually those behaviours which would be counter-productive to effective performance at any level in the job.

This form of levelling is usually used where a framework relates to a single job grade or role. It does not, therefore, represent degrees of job difficulty so much as degrees of individual competency. Consequently, it would be common to find this type of framework alongside other frameworks for different job levels in the same organisation.

This method was often used to assess different degrees of competency in a group of individuals. For example: when assessing job applicants, the threshold behavioural indicators could be used; when assessing job performance of experienced staff, the outstanding competencies could be used. In both cases the negative indicators may have played a part in identifying disqualifying factors or development needs. Generally, a well-designed rating system can produce the same results, without the need for a multiple competency framework. See Chapters 4 (**Using Competencies in Selection**) and 5 (**Using Competencies to Review Performance**) for more information.

Competency titles and descriptions

To help with communication, competencies are usually given a title and some form of description. The competency title is usually very short and distinguishes the competency from other competencies while being descriptive and easy to remember.

Typical examples of competency titles are:

managing relationships

teamworking

influencing

gathering and analysing information

decision-making

personal development

generating and building on ideas

planning and organising

deadline management

objective-setting.

In addition to the competency title, many frameworks include competency descriptions. There are two main approaches to competency descriptions. The first approach is to summarise the behaviours contained within the competency. For example, a competency such as 'Planning and organising' may be summarised as:

Achieves results through detailed planning and organisation of people and resources to meet goals, targets or objectives within agreed timescales.

Where competencies summarise a single list of behaviours this approach works very well.

The second approach is to provide a rationale for the competency in place of a summary – ie a description of why the competency is important to the organisation. This works well where competency frameworks contain levels of behaviours, because in these cases it is difficult to produce a summary that would cover all roles in the organisation and all behaviours within the competency.

For example, in the **Appendix Framework** (see page 133) the competency 'GROWS BUSINESS CAPABILITY: Improvement Focus' has three levels. Each has its own brief definition:

Level 1 promotes a business-wide culture of continuous improvement
Level 2 facilitates improvements within teams and across departments
Level 3 contributes and encourages others to contribute to new ideas.

Instead of trying to summarise all the levels in one definition, we produced the following:

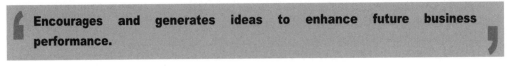

> **Encourages and generates ideas to enhance future business performance.**

In many ways this statement is more useful than a competency summary as it indicates why the organisation values the competency as well as giving a flavour of what the competency covers.

Competency clusters

A competency cluster is a collection of closely related competencies, usually three to five per cluster. Most competency frameworks have clusters of competencies relating to:

- thinking – eg analysing and deciding
- acting – eg achieving results
- interacting – eg working with people.

This form of clustering can seem dry and academic. Some organisations deliberately cluster competencies to say something important about what the organisation is trying to achieve. The latter approach has been used in the **Appendix Framework** (see page 132) referred to throughout this book. The clusters, and their competencies, are:

- SHOWS THE WAY

  DIRECTION: uses accurate business knowledge to achieve common goals
  LEADERSHIP: provides clear leadership consistent with our vision, mission and values
  PLANNING: sets and agrees plans for self and/or others based on business goals.

- GROWS BUSINESS CAPABILITY

  IMPROVEMENT FOCUS: encourages and generates ideas to enhance future business performance
  BUSINESS FOCUS: uses understanding of the business to improve results
  CUSTOMER FOCUS: uses understanding of the needs of customers to drive action.

- GROWS INDIVIDUAL CAPABILITY

  DEVELOPING: demonstrates trust and confidence in the ability of others
  MANAGING PERFORMANCE: inspires ownership and achievement of standards.

Phrases such as these indicate the priorities of the organisation. Some organisations also provide cluster descriptions to indicate the nature of the competencies contained within each cluster. This is not usually needed with small frameworks, as most users will be focusing on the the competencies rather than the clusters. However, to illustrate the point, 'SHOWS THE WAY' (a cluster from the **Appendix Framework** (see page 132) could be described thus:

> **Keeps activity within the business focused on its common local and strategic goals by providing appropriate plans and clear leadership.**

Competency framework

'Competency framework' is the term given to the complete collection of clusters, competencies (with or without levels) and behavioural indicators.

The number of competencies within frameworks continues to decline. While it is still possible to find frameworks that contain 30 or more competencies, most users find between 8 and 12 competencies in a single framework to be sufficient. In order to cover a range of different job groups, some organisations operate several competency frameworks at the same time.

Where *each* competency in a framework relates to *all* jobs in an organisation or department, the framework is unlikely to contain all the competencies needed for each job. This type of competency framework only contains competencies common to all jobs, and is often referred to as a 'core competency framework'. Frameworks of this type will contain fewer competencies than frameworks that contain *all* the competencies needed for *all* jobs. This latter type of framework is effectively a library from which the competencies relevant to specific jobs can be selected. For some applications, job profiles based on core competencies may need supplementing with additional job-specific competencies.

Large, complex and detailed frameworks spell out exactly what is required for all applications and all roles. Such frameworks can be unwieldy because they have to describe behaviours in great detail and often cannot cater for minor variations between similar jobs. The detail also means that such frameworks quickly become out of date as jobs change. Human resource staff in such organisations will have a time-consuming role not only updating the framework, but also monitoring usage to ensure the framework is being used properly.

In organisations where line managers actively take responsibility for people management, our experience has shown that it is more effective to produce a generic framework with broad behavioural indicators, such as our **Appendix Framework** (see page 132), with guidelines and support for users on how to adapt and use it for different applications. A generic framework may take more time to roll out, particularly the training of managers in how to use it effectively. However, such frameworks are much more easily adapted to local practices, are easier to administer and stay relevant for longer.

Example framework

This structure, with competency clusters as the highest elements and behavioural indicators as the most detailed elements, remains one of the most common layouts for a competency framework. The **Appendix Framework** is structured in this way. Figure 2 illustrates this, using examples from the SHOWS THE WAY cluster.

COMPETENCY CLUSTER: SHOWS THE WAY

COMPETENCIES *with levels*

■ DIRECTION

Level 1: develops strategies that account for the short-, medium- and long-term needs of the business

Level 2: keeps others informed of business goals and inspires buy-in to them

Level 3: supports business goals by addressing issues likely to affect achieving them.

■ LEADERSHIP

Level 1: is consistent in expectations of others and provides clear leadership

Level 2: operates openly, is accessible and approachable to others.

■ PLANNING

Level 1: ensures business plans are achievable and integrated with business goals

Level 2: ensures plans meet local needs and that they account for the needs of other teams

Level 3: uses appropriate planning to succeed in own role.

BEHAVIOURAL INDICATORS (for Direction)

Level 1: Develops strategies that account for the short-, medium- and long-term needs of the business	Level 2: Keeps others informed of business goals and inspires buy-in to them	Level 3: Supports business goals by addressing issues likely to affect achieving them
■ Produces and regularly communicates three- to five-year plans to ensure strategies remain relevant ■ Balances long-term goals with short-term deliverables to achieve business goals ■ Ensures business goals are communicated and understood across the business.	■ Develops local goals to support wider business goals ■ Inspires buy-in to business goals by showing how individual efforts contribute to them ■ Provides timely and appropriate information to support achievement of business goals.	■ Focuses and encourages others to focus on delivering the business goals ■ Regularly reviews and communicates progress on business goals ■ Uses the business goals to prioritise work.

Figure 2 *Typical content of a competency framework*

QUALITIES OF GOOD COMPETENCY FRAMEWORKS

For a competency framework to be effective it must be usable and fit for its intended purpose. To be fit for its purpose a competency framework should at least conform to the quality standards listed in Table 2. In the first edition of this book we provided a list of five quality standards. Due to problems we have been asked to address, with competency frameworks established by others, we have introduced two additional quality standards to our previous list. These are 'elements should be of the same type' and 'behaviours should be necessary and appropriate'.

The quality standards outlined in Table 2 (below) provide a good basis for evaluating and testing a framework – during or after its production. Where a framework fails on a standard it will usually be possible to correct the problem. However, correction is not always easy or cost-effective, which is why it is better to use the standards to check a framework while it is being developed, rather than when it is in its final draft. Frameworks that do not meet the quality standards, and that are not corrected, are at best not going to be the good management tool they could be and, at worst, will be damaging to the organisation.

Each of the quality standards for a good competency framework is explored below.

Clear and easy to understand

A clear and easy-to-understand competency framework should:

- be unambiguous
- use simple language
- have a simple structure
- have a logical structure.

To be clear and easy to understand a competency framework should reflect the language and phrases commonly used within the organisation. The framework should also be structured and presented in a way that is easy for its users to follow.

Competency frameworks that are unclear or difficult to use are frustrating to use and are likely to be abandoned.

Relevant

The language used in the framework has to be relevant to all the people who are going to use it, whether the framework is generic or specific. 'Relevant to all people' means that job-holders should recognise the

Table 2

QUALITY STANDARDS FOR COMPETENCY FRAMEWORKS
■ clear and easy to understand
■ relevant to all people who will be affected by the framework
■ takes account of expected changes
■ has discrete elements (eg behavioural indicators do not overlap)
■ elements should be of the same type
■ behaviours should be necessary and appropriate
■ fair to all affected by its use.

behavioural indicators as examples of behaviours necessary for effective performance in their jobs. In addition, everybody who will use, or be affected by, the framework should be able to see the relevance to the application(s).

In generic frameworks, relevance has to be across all roles; in specific frameworks, relevance may be limited to particular roles or applications.

Relevant to all roles – generic frameworks

Maximum use can be made of competency frameworks when they are relevant to all roles in an organisation or department. 'Relevant to all roles' means that the competencies must describe, in generic terms, groups of related behaviours that are essential for effective performance in all roles covered by the framework. It is essential that behavioural indicators have direct relevance to the effective tackling of actual job demands within the appropriate organisational context.

Relevant to the application or role – specific frameworks

Where competencies are being developed for a specific application or role, the competency framework should be relevant to that application or role. For example, a competency framework produced specifically for selection must have a sufficient number of detailed behavioural indicators to allow assessors to recognise appropriate examples of competency during the assessment process. This point is covered in detail in Chapter 4 (**Using Competencies in Selection**).

Takes account of expected changes

If a competency framework is to stay relevant, it must take account of expected changes that are likely to affect the way in which the organisation operates. These changes are incorporated into competency frameworks by including behaviours that describe the way individuals will need to go about their jobs in the short- to medium-term future.

Insights into future-oriented behaviours will often come from the vision of the future that the leaders of the organisation are using to set targets and plans. Finally, for a competency framework to stay relevant, it must be kept up to date and take account of:

- changes in the organisation's environment
- the introduction of new technology
- changes in the vision of the future, which leaders are using to inform their decisions.

Discrete elements

One of the main uses for competencies is as criteria in assessment. This may be assessment for selection or assessment for performance appraisal or assessment for succession. The structure of a competency framework will have a major influence on the ease and accuracy of assessments. To avoid assessing the same performance more than once, elements of the competencies must not be replicated within the framework. Otherwise, it will be difficult for assessors to know to which competency they should assign an example of performance. A few simple rules, such as those below, can be used to avoid confusion in the application of competencies:

- One competency must not depend on another competency – eg a person should not have to be good at one competency in order to be good at another competency within the same framework.
- Competencies and indicators must appear in only one place in the framework – eg a behavioural indicator in one competency should not be reproduced or paraphrased in another competency.
- Competencies must not relate to more than one cluster.

■ Competencies must be distinct from each other. The more competencies there are in a framework the less distinct from each other they will be.

Behavioural indicators are the detailed and working part of the competency. To help to ensure that the behavioural indicators are capable of doing their job, they should:

■ relate to only one competency

■ relate to only one competency level

■ describe directly measurable (ie observable) examples of an individual's competency – for example:

    ■ *keeps colleagues informed of changes to work priorities*

    ■ *produces detailed plans for achieving objectives.*

■ describe just one piece of behaviour or evidence – generally, it should not be possible for an individual to be good at one part of the indicator and poor at another. There are a few exceptions to this rule. In a generic framework some behaviours may have 'and/or' statements to cover different possibilities. For example, 'sets SMART objectives for self and/or team' is valid, because it applies to everyone, whether they have a team or not. In addition, there may be behaviours that are so interlinked the behaviour would not be valid if only one part was observed. For example, 'writes accurate reports in a readable format'. Although it would be possible for someone to write an accurate report in an unreadable format, this would not be desirable. The degree of detail depends on the use to which the behaviours are being applied. More information about this will be covered in the following chapters

■ include an action: indicators describe what a person does – eg:

    ■ *keeps colleagues informed* of changes to work priorities

    ■ *produces detailed plans* for achieving objectives.

■ include enough contextual information to make the action meaningful – ie indicate why the person is performing the action – eg:

    ■ keeps colleagues informed *of changes to work priorities*

    ■ produces detailed plans *for achieving objectives.*

Elements should be of the same type

The basic building-blocks of competencies are behaviours. All aspects of the competency framework should therefore be behaviour-based. However, many competency frameworks mix together behaviours and personal characteristics such as knowledge, motives and abilities. Having the right knowledge, motives and abilities does not mean that an individual can use these effectively when faced with the demands of a particular job in a given organisational context.

Mixing behaviours, knowledge, motives and abilities creates a great deal of confusion, especially when the competencies are used in assessments. Some things will be measured several times during the assessment and the results will be impossible to interpret meaningfully.

Ineffective communication

An organisation created a competency framework which included a competency called 'Communication'. When it came to assessment against this in recruitment exercises, assessors found it hard to know how to rate it. For example, someone displaying the competency 'teamworking' was doing so partly because they were good at communication. The same person was also using communication when demonstrating the competency 'influencing'.

Assessors were therefore being invited to rate teamworking and communication using one piece of evidence. They were also being invited to rate 'influencing' and 'communication' using another piece of evidence. This would result in four scores from two pieces of evidence.

This competency framework would fail on two of our quality standards. Firstly, the elements are not discrete. Performance on 'influencing' and performance on 'teamworking' are dependent on 'communication' performance. Secondly, elements are not of the same type. Communication is an ability that enables performance, whereas 'influencing' and 'teamworking' refer to behaviours.

Communication is frequently included in competency frameworks – in fact it was the second most popular 'competency' as reported in the annual *Competency & Emotional Intelligence* survey (2002). However, communication is an ability that influences many aspects of behaviour; it is not a competency.

Behaviours should be necessary and appropriate

Competency frameworks should be designed to help enhance individual performance; they should not compensate for poor practice within the organisation. Poor procedures and dangerous practices should be corrected by addressing the procedures and practices directly. The behaviours within a competency framework should be the behaviours necessary for effective performance when a job-holder is working with appropriate procedures and safe practices.

Fair to all

A framework could meet the above quality standards, but still institutionalise and inadvertently encourage unfair biases in organisations. This can occur when insufficient attention has been paid to potential sources of bias – eg a management competency framework compiled using data collected only from older, white, male managers may exclude behaviours that could be observed in effective managers who do not come from this sample.

Checklist

A checklist of the qualities of a good competency framework is provided in **Appendix 2**. Readers can use this to check:

- if an existing framework needs updating
- the qualities of a new framework during development
- that a newly developed framework is ready for launch.

KEY POINTS

- A competency framework is a set of performance criteria.

- Competencies provide a common foundation for a range of people-management activities and processes.
- Competencies need to be structured to aid their use.
- Typical competency frameworks contain the following elements:
    - behavioural indicators: the detailed statements that make up competencies
    - competencies: lists of related behavioural indicators
    - clusters: groups of related competencies.
- A 'competency' may be made up of one or more lists of related behavioural indicators.
- Competencies made of more than one list of behavioural indicators are referred to as 'levelled' competencies.
- Competencies can be levelled using job grades, complexity-of-job demands or expected degrees of job-holder competency.
- Competencies levelled by complexity-of-job demand are the most practical.
- Good competency frameworks will have *all* of the following qualities:
    - clear and easy to understand
    - relevant to all who will be affected by them
    - account for expected changes
    - made up of discrete elements
    - elements will be of the same type
    - behaviours are both necessary and appropriate
    - fair towards all actual or potential jobholders.
- It is much easier to implement and manage a generic framework with clear user guidelines than it is to try to make a framework cover the detail of all roles and all applications.
- A checklist of the qualities of a good competency framework is provided in Appendix 2.

REFERENCES AND READING

RANKIN N. (2002) *Competency & Emotional Intelligence*. 'Benchmarking Survey' (Benchmarking edition) 2002. pp2–22.

Developing competency frameworks

In the Introduction we mentioned that the primary reason for developing competency frameworks is to provide an explicit link between business objectives and people-management policies and practices. In other words, competency frameworks are tools to enhance individual and organisational performance – and not, as some may believe, to keep HR professionals in a job! Some organisations are developing their first competency framework, others are already using one, but wish to update it or enhance it. This chapter outlines best practice in the development of frameworks for the organisation new to competencies, and for those that wish to extend, update or adapt their existing framework.

In this chapter we discuss three key principles that any development work involving competency frameworks should take into account. These are:

1   Involve the people who will be affected by the framework.
2   Keep people informed about what is happening and why.
3   Create competencies that are relevant.

We then outline five ways in which a competency framework might be developed. These are:

1   Developing a generic framework from scratch – where no framework exists
2   Extending an existing framework – to incorporate a wider range of jobs
3   Updating a framework – to ensure the existing framework remains relevant
4   Developing a specific framework from scratch – to address needs such as development or performance management in a particular area of the organisation
5   Adapting an existing framework to meet specific needs – to tailor an existing framework for needs in a particular part of the organisation or for a particular application.

The section on how to develop a generic framework from scratch is the template for all design work. The remaining sections show how this basic design template can be adapted to meet other competency framework development needs.

It is often argued that all competency frameworks contain the same basic structure and very similar competencies. Therefore, it is also argued, it should be possible to take an existing framework and 'tweak' it. However, it takes a lot more than a tweak to make an off-the-shelf competency framework effective. Even when a competency framework is imposed by another part of an organisation, every effort needs to be made to customise the framework to meet the needs of its local users and to ensure that it meets the quality standards outlined in Chapter 2 (**A Typical Competency Framework**).

Production of a competency framework requires structure and discipline, which this chapter will help to provide. Competency design also requires some specialist skills. This chapter will not make readers experts in competency design, so specialist skills may need to be acquired and/or brought in if they are not available within the organisation.

The 80:20 principle applies when producing, extending, updating or adapting a competency framework. Invest 80 per cent of your effort in careful planning, development and roll-out of the competencies, and you will be rewarded with a framework that is an invaluable management tool requiring minimal maintenance. However, spend only 20 per cent of your effort upfront and it is virtually guaranteed that you will spend a significantly greater proportion of your time amending the framework and trying to make it work. Spending too little time upfront can result in a framework that is useless or even damaging to the organisation. It simply isn't worth skimping on the design and production of a competency framework.

Regardless of whether a completely new framework is being produced or an existing framework extended, updated or adapted, it is important to remember that the intended users need to feel ownership of the framework and be able to see its relevance. Ownership and relevance can be achieved if certain key principles are followed while producing the competency framework, and if a disciplined process is employed for producing it.

KEY PRINCIPLES FOR PRODUCING COMPETENCIES

Three key principles must be followed when producing, extending, updating or adapting a competency framework in order to ensure ownership and relevance for its users. These principles will also help to meet the quality standards described in Chapter 2 (**A Typical Competency Framework**).

1 Involve the people who will be affected by the framework.
2 Keep people informed about what is happening and why.
3 Create competencies that are relevant to all those who will be affected by them as well as to organisational needs and intended applications.

Failure to adhere to these principles means that commitment to the competencies could be minimal or non-existent.

Key principle 1 – involve people

The views held by potential users will influence their enthusiasm for the competencies, so organisations should find out what these views are *before* the competencies have been finalised. Involving potential users in producing the competencies ensures that users' views can be sought while demonstrating that the framework belongs to the users.

A sensitive situation

A public utility was introducing major changes to supervisory roles. The change process included the identification of competencies for the new supervisor role and the assessment of existing supervisors against these competencies. As a result of the assessments some job-holders would be offered regrading or a move to a non-supervisory role. The situation was very sensitive.

Before the competencies were produced, everybody who would be affected by them was informed about the business need for producing them and how they would be used. In addition, representatives from the relevant groups were involved in providing information and in reviewing the competencies as they were being developed. Despite the sensitivities, the competencies were accepted by all who would be affected by them, including union representatives.

What about us?

Recently, an insurance company experienced difficulty getting a new competency framework implemented. Potential users questioned the relevance of the competencies to their business area. When challenged, they criticised the wording and structure of the competencies. To explore this further, potential users were interviewed.

The message from the interviewees was very clear: potential users felt that the competencies were being imposed on them. The strong criticisms this group made about the competencies were their way of demonstrating their objections to this imposition. In this way they were obstructing the introduction of the framework.

The first situation involved everybody likely to be affected by the competencies in the production of those competencies. In the second situation, competencies had been developed by a small group within the corporate business, which then asked the operating businesses to introduce them locally. In the first situation users were involved, whereas the second situation alienated the users.

It is not necessary to involve every potential user in every stage when producing a competency framework. Involvement should at least seek to include individuals from different areas of the business who might champion the framework. It is also crucial that potential critics and individuals sensitive to the successful implementation of a competency framework are involved.

Key principle 2 – keep people informed

Everybody with an interest in the competency framework – whether or not they are yet aware of this – needs to be kept informed as to:

- why it is being produced – in particular, how it will help people in their work and career, and how it will benefit the organisation
- how it is going to be produced
- how it is intended to be used.

To communicate this, some or all of the following points will need to be considered:

- what will happen – ie key activities such as data-gathering interviews, meetings, testing drafts
- why these activities are necessary
- when the key activities will take place
- what is expected of the people in the organisation
- what individuals' roles in the design process will be, including project team members and consultants, if used
- why individuals have been asked to make a particular contribution – eg as an interviewee
- why individuals may not have been asked to make a particular contribution
- whom to contact for further information.

The degree to which an individual is to be involved in the production process will determine how much that person needs to know.

Good communication removes potential obstacles to producing competencies and reduces or eliminates difficulties at implementation. For example, producing competencies requires the collection of job information. A great deal of this information will be collected from job-holders. It is easier to gain the co-operation of job-holders when they know why information is being collected and what their role is in providing this information. When people are asked to provide something without knowing why it is needed, individuals tend to produce their own explanations, often assuming the worst. It is hard to collect objective information about a job when job-holders believe their performance is being assessed or that jobs may change dramatically as a result of the interview.

It can 'end in tears'

Several years ago a consultant went to interview job-holders as part of a project for producing competencies. That week, in another part of the organisation, there had been some redundancy announcements. Unfortunately, the organisation did not inform interviewees about the purpose of the interviews or brief the consultant about the redundancy situation. Interviewees were suspicious about the real purpose of the interviews and started to draw their own conclusions.

The consultant's first interview lasted only a few minutes – the interviewee did not co-operate and ended the interview by throwing paperwork against the wall and walking out.

Fortunately, such extremes of poor communication and such strong reactions are very rare.

Key principle 3 – create competencies that are relevant

Relevant competencies are those that describe behaviours that can be applied to all the jobs that the competency framework is intended to cover. An organisation-wide framework will describe broad generic behaviours. However, these behaviours must be relevant to all users of the framework. For example, in the **Appendix Framework** (see page 133), one of the behaviours in 'GROWS BUSINESS CAPABILITY: Business Focus, Level 1' is 'Monitors external environment to minimise its negative impact on business results.' This is a generic behaviour that can apply to managers wherever they work in the organisation. The HR manager may be looking at the 'external environment' in terms of the local and national employment situation and changing employment legislation. The sales manager may be looking at the 'external environment' in terms of competitors' sales.

Behavioural descriptions in competencies must be relevant to all actual and potential job-holders covered by the scope of the framework, irrespective of non-job-related criteria such as sex, age or race.

If any behavioural indicators include statements about physical ability, it is important that they are absolutely necessary. Assumptions cannot be made about physical characteristics required to undertake tasks. Requirements for specific physical characteristics will need to be checked with experts during the design process.

Avoiding unfairness

A water company was developing core competencies for a group of operational roles. In analysing these roles, such phrases as 'physically agile' were generated from interviews. Although this characteristic was relevant to particular aspects of some of the jobs being analysed (eg surveying construction sites), it was certainly not relevant to all jobs. Including the characteristic could have resulted in unfair discrimination when recruiting for jobs that did not require the characteristic. The behaviour was therefore not included in the framework.

The work done on developing the competency framework had identified that physical disability was not a restriction on effective performance in many roles. A positive consequence of this was that the organisation no longer considered physical disabilities a bar to selection for the majority of existing roles.

Finally, competency frameworks can quickly become obsolete. It is essential that competencies are at least relevant on the day of their launch and preferable that they remain relevant for as long as possible afterwards. To achieve this it is essential that a vision of the future is encompassed when developing a competency framework. In considering relevance, current and expected demands must be balanced with expected changes.

PRODUCING A GENERIC COMPETENCY FRAMEWORK FROM SCRATCH

The following key steps capture the main activities for developing a competency framework from scratch:

- preparation
- collecting information
- compiling the framework
- rolling out the framework.

These steps are described below and all three key principles need to be considered within each step. Where specialist skills are required, these are mentioned.

Preparation

It is important that this project is led from within the organisation. Even if most of the project team is made up of external consultants, they must be seen to be supporting the project and not leading it themselves.

There are four main considerations when preparing to produce a competency framework:

- getting buy-in from key people
- clarification of purpose
- planning the project
- putting a data-gathering/analysis team together.

Getting buy-in from key people

Everybody with a potential stake in the success or failure of the competency framework needs to be 'bought in' to its production. Buy-in includes a commitment to resourcing the production of the competency framework as well as commitment to using the competencies.

It is essential that competencies are developed as a business tool – a device to help the management of performance within the business. Potential users and investors in competencies need to be made aware of the benefits that competencies will bring. A statement of the need for a framework, and clarification about how competencies will help fill this need, must be developed in order to argue this case.

Remember that buy-in must include commitment to the roll-out of the competency framework and to keeping it up to date.

Management buy-in

A major brewing company introduced a competency framework for its executive management roles as part of an initiative to develop closer links and a common identity across the business. The brewery company had grown over the years, acquiring a number of operating sites. As a result, each site tended to have its own way of doing things and its own identity. The HR director worked with other board members to identify a way of unifying the attitudes and behaviours of executive managers across the different sites. A competency framework was considered a key tool to achieve this because it would provide managers with a consistent model of the behaviours necessary within their roles. In this example, buy-in was obtained at the highest level.

Buy-in was also obtained from the executive managers. This was achieved by presenting a clear business case for the need to unify attitudes and behaviours, and by openly demonstrating the commitment which board members were making to the project. One example of this commitment was the inclusion of board members in the competency framework production team. Another example was in the involvement of all board members in communications about the project. Overall, the proposal to produce and use competencies was always talked about in business terms. Although the initiative was inspired from within HR, the project was not seen as being owned by that function. From the outset the project was presented and seen as a business need, driven from all business areas.

The above example demonstrates that obtaining buy-in and clarifying the purpose are very likely to occur together.

Clarification of the purpose

The critical issue about clarification of purpose is that the purpose of the competency framework will influence what the competencies look like and how they can be used. For example:

- Competencies for selection must be relevant to a particular vacancy and will be specific to a few roles, describing what is similar about them.
- Job-grading competencies must cover all jobs/roles in the grading scheme and need to indicate how they differ.
- Succession planning competencies must indicate how jobs are similar as well as how they differ.

Behaviours required for competencies designed specifically for one application may make them very difficult to use for other applications. To be manageable, a competency framework to cover all roles and support all people-management processes will usually contain generic behavioural indicators that may need adapting for specific applications.

As stated, some degree of clarity of purpose will have taken place before buy-in has been achieved. However, in our experience the intended purpose may change while buy-in is being sought – involving others means taking account of their views. For example, stakeholders may identify new potential applications that the proposers had not. Some negotiation should be expected, therefore, between proposing to produce a competency framework and commitment to develop it.

It is possible to collect specific information for all roles and all intended applications in the process of producing a competency framework. To do so will require significant time and resources for the project, particularly the data-gathering and data-analysis stages. A far more preferable solution is to produce a generic competency framework with user and application guidelines – outlining how users should gather more detailed information or adapt competencies for a specific application when required. This approach has the added advantages of encouraging greater understanding and ownership of the competency framework by its users.

Everybody who is to be involved in the production of the competency framework must have a common understanding of its purpose and very similar views of what it is likely to look like. One way to test the understanding of those involved is to ask them to describe what they think the competency framework might look like when it is completed. It will not be possible at this stage to have complete agreement on the likely appearance of the framework, but significant differences must be addressed. When examining why organisations have had difficulty in making competency frameworks work, we often find that different users have had different expectations of what was going to be produced. They also had no reason to suspect that what would be produced would not be what they wanted.

Somebody was bound to be disappointed

An insurance company was developing a competency framework. One group with a particular interest in selection was expecting a competency framework based on behavioural indicators. Another group of users was planning to start skill-based training programmes and was expecting a set of task-based competencies. Each group of users knew what they meant by competencies – it was just that each group did not want the type of competencies the other group wanted. In addition, the team who were developing the competency framework had their own view of how the framework would be used – ie its purpose.

The user groups had not made their expectations or needs explicit to the development team. The development team did not communicate its views about purpose to the users. Inevitably, the final framework could not adequately fulfil the purposes for which the user groups had intended to use it.

Planning the project

Producing a competency framework can be a lengthy process involving many people and many different activities. Careful and comprehensive planning is therefore essential. Inadequate planning for collecting information is probably the most common cause of delays when developing competency frameworks.

Planning should be led by someone who fully understands the detailed activities in each step of the production process. Where possible, the data gathering analysis team should be involved in the planning to increase their understanding and buy-in to the project.

Effective plans should ensure that:

- potential obstacles are identified and their effects minimised or eliminated
- communication is focused on progress and achievements
- possible delays are identified and contingencies are in place to deal with them.

The planning stage provides an excellent opportunity to incorporate all three 'key principles', described earlier, into every step of the project.

Here is a guide to how each of the key principles might be applied:

- *Involve the people who will be affected by the framework*
  - Identify everybody who will be affected by the competency framework and consider how and when they need to be involved in the project.
  - Ensure that the right people are available at the right times.
  - Build in flexibility for rearranging interviews, etc.

- *Keep people informed about what is happening and why*
  - Consider what needs to be communicated; who needs to be communicated to; when to communicate; what the best media are for communicating different messages.
  - As with the first key principle, apply these considerations to each stage.
  - Don't forget lead times for the production and distribution of communication material.

- *Create competencies that are relevant.*
  - Always refer to the intended purpose of the competency framework when planning each stage of the project.
  - Ensure that relevant techniques are used to collect appropriate information for compiling the competency framework.

It is also worth considering how the framework will be managed and kept up to date after it has been launched. There are three reasons for considering this when planning:

- The process for ongoing monitoring of the framework may indicate who to involve in the various stages of the production project.

  For example, different departments may need a representative in charge of identifying changes required in the framework. These individuals could be identified and included in the project at an early stage. This will encourage ownership as well as a thorough understanding of the framework and its intended purposes.

- How the framework will be kept up to date, and who by, should be considered – especially if the framework covers the whole organisation.

  Issues such as the production and distribution of updates should also be considered. Without one point of control, the newly launched framework is in danger of evolving into many 'tailored' versions as each part of the organisation updates it with changes. Try to identify and involve this person at appropriate points in the plan.

■ Explaining that there will be a system for updating the framework, and outlining how people may input to that process, will help buy-in when the framework is launched. All staff should know that the final framework is not 'set in stone' for ever.

The updating process must be communicated carefully. The process should not be interpreted by the audience as an excuse for launching a poor framework, nor should it suggest that the framework is never quite finished.

Putting the data-gathering/analysis team together

Ideally, the data-gathering team should be made up of individuals from all areas of the organisation who will use the framework. The members of the data-gathering team will also form the data-analysis team. All team members will take on the role of job analysts and therefore need to be skilled in job-analysis techniques. Where there is an insufficient number of suitable organisational staff available, organisations frequently rely on external experts.

A very effective compromise in the make-up of the data-gathering team is to combine internal staff with external experts. There can be particular advantages to using external experts in some parts of the data-gathering. Work required in sensitive areas within the organisation – for example, where major changes are under way – and any work involving senior managers or board members is often delegated to external experts.

It is essential to check the credentials and expertise of external experts. For example, speak to past clients and review examples of similar work that they have personally been involved in. Check that they have the same clarity of understanding of what you are trying to produce. The quality standards checklist in **Appendix 2** could be used to test their views on what makes a good framework.

It is also important that all members of the design team (including any external consultants) fully understand and agree what they mean by competency. This clarity of understanding should be checked before any work is undertaken, and a common understanding agreed.

Four to eight job analysts, depending on the diversity of roles and the size of the organisation, will make an effective-size a team. Ideally, teams should be restricted to a maximum of eight analysts, as this makes the data-gathering and subsequent analysis easier to manage.

Team membership should, where possible, represent the diversity of people in the organisation by, for example, sex, ethnic grouping and age. It is also essential that everybody in the team is trained and skilled in the use of all the data-gathering techniques to be employed during the project. When job analysts are involved in using all the data-gathering techniques they develop a more rounded view of the organisation and the demands its jobs place on job-holders. This is particularly useful when the team come together with all the data and begin to try to make sense of it at the analysis stage.

It helps the data-analysis process if team members are able to deal with ambiguity in the use of language and have good verbal reasoning skills. At the analysis stage, team members will be grouping together what they consider to be related behaviours. Anyone who has difficulty in identifying alternative interpretations for some statements is likely to find data analysis – which can involve reviewing thousands of statements – a bit too challenging.

Collecting information

This is usually the most lengthy and time-consuming part of the production process. Once again the three key principles for developing competencies need to be borne in mind. Individuals will need to be involved as providers of information about their jobs or jobs they manage or by identifying expected changes that will affect the way people do their work. Individuals will need to be informed about how they will make their contribution and about the types of techniques that they will encounter. The choice of job-analysis techniques and individuals to provide information will influence the relevance of the competencies.

Collecting information requires particular attention to three things:

- choosing analysis techniques
- data-gathering
- preparing data for analysis.

Choosing analysis techniques

There is a wide variety of techniques specifically designed for collecting information about jobs and work. These techniques fall within the area of job analysis. Every technique has its pros and cons:

- No single technique is sufficient for all data collection.
- Not all techniques for analysing jobs suit all situations.

For example, observation techniques work very well for jobs that contain manual activities, but they are not well suited to analysing mental activities such as thinking or reasoning. In addition, the structure or politics within an organisation might dictate a particular approach. For example, it is sometimes necessary to interview certain people only because leaving them out could undermine future use of the competencies. In this situation it is better to provide a structure for the individuals' contribution than to leave them to make unstructured and uninformed criticisms.

It is good practice when producing a competency framework to use three or four different job-analysis techniques in combination. This helps to provide a checking device for the data – preventing irrelevant and atypical behaviours being incorporated into the competency framework. A typical combination of techniques would be:

- structured one-to-one interviews
- questionnaires
- group sessions.

For example, when collecting information about the future direction of an organisation, a visioning workshop with members of the board and senior managers might be used. When collecting information about important activities within jobs, structured techniques such as interviews or questionnaires are more effective. To identify where jobs are similar or different, group sessions with job-holders and job-holders' managers may be the most effective. The combination of different techniques and different people also enables the analysts to see whether different sources agree about the demands and behaviours needed for the target jobs.

Avoid combining techniques that only look at the characteristics of successful people, as these can be misleading. Success is not always based on effective performance in a job. Individuals, for example, who are successful in employing political skills to succeed in organisations may have similar characteristics. However, these may not be the characteristics that the organisation needs or wishes to promote. It is essential when choosing job-analysis techniques that the techniques enable reported behaviours to be traced back to necessary and appropriate job demands.

Although some techniques are easy to learn and easy to use, *all* techniques require training and practice before they can be used effectively.

Data-gathering

The main objectives for data-gathering are:

- to collect examples of behaviours needed for effective performance in the jobs to be covered by the competency framework
- to identify behaviours that will be necessary for effective performance in these jobs in the future.

It is important that all relevant information is gathered. Some information can be taken from existing documents; other information must be collected from individuals. Sources of data include:

- business plans
- strategy documents
- statements of organisational principles and/or values
- examples of what job-holders do
- examples of what job-holders produce
- job-holders' views about their own jobs
- managers' views about the work of job-holders
- subordinates views about the work of job-holders
- training documentation
- job descriptions
- regulatory information and legal requirements
- customers' and suppliers' views about the organisation
- customers' and suppliers' views about the employees of the organisation
- specialists with knowledge of the job as it is – eg trainers
- specialists who have knowledge of how jobs will change – eg IT experts
- executive and senior management views about the future
- external experts' views about the future – eg sector specialists/analysts.

The type of data to collect will be influenced by the intended purpose of the competency framework. For a generic competency framework, broad descriptions of behaviour taken from a wide range of examples of effective performance are needed. A framework that is to be used for a particular application needs to contain data more specific to the intended application. In both cases, information about the direction of the business and a wide range of examples of effective behaviours needs to be collected.

Table 3 describes the level of data-gathering required when producing a competency framework.

Not all job-holders need to be included in this stage. There will be an opportunity to involve more of them in the later stage of 'validating the draft framework'.

To ensure that the competency framework will be relevant throughout an organisation it is important to collect information about jobs right across the organisation. For example, to create a generic competency framework a sample of jobs should be analysed from each department or function and a sample of jobs

Table 3 *The level of data-gathering required when describing behavioural indicators*

		APPLICATION	
		Specific	**General**
J O B	**Specific**	*eg recruitment for all team leaders* Gather data: ❑ specific to the application ❑ within the identified jobs/roles ❑ from the relevant business unit(s).	*eg all applications, for all team leaders* Gather data: ❑ relevant to all applications ❑ within the identified jobs/roles ❑ from the relevant business unit(s).
R O L E	**General**	*eg recruitment for all jobs* Gather data: ❑ specific to the application ❑ across all jobs/roles ❑ across the whole organisation.	*eg all applications, for all jobs* Gather data: ❑ relevant to all applications ❑ across all jobs/roles ❑ across the whole organisation.

Table 4 *Example of sampling methodology for data-gathering in a large organisation*

Roles / Functions	Marketing	Sales	Production	Distribution	Packaging	Personnel	Finance
Senior managers	▨		▨		▨		▨
Middle managers		▨		▨		▨	
Junior managers	▨		▨		▨		▨
Team leaders		▨		▨		▨	
Administrative staff	▨		▨		▨		▨
Operational staff		▨		▨		▨	

should be analysed across all roles (eg administration, operations, technical, management). One form of sampling is to take a series of diagonal slices through the organisation, as in Table 4.

For each shaded box two things usually take place:

■ Information will be collected from a selection of job-holders about their own jobs.

- A selection of line managers for roles in the shaded boxes will be asked to identify behaviours that differentiate good performance from less good performance among their direct reports.

In addition:

- A sample of job-holders from each horizontal slice of the organisation (ie with similar roles in different functions) could be brought together in group sessions. These groups might identify similarities and differences between jobs at their level across the organisation.

- Changes likely to affect how people go about their work could be explored using interviews and/or workshops. These sessions would be likely to include senior managers and other individuals with knowledge of imminent changes.

The sample of job-holders who contribute to the data-gathering should represent the diversity of people that do or could occupy jobs in the organisation by, for example, age, sex or ethnic group. Where this is not possible it may be necessary to supplement the job-analysis data with views from appropriate experts.

The number of job-holders that will be involved during this data-gathering stage depends on how different or similar roles are across the organisation. The more differences there are between roles, the greater the number of people needed in the sample. So, for instance, organisations with a wide range of technical specialists might need to include a large sample of job-holders. Where roles are very similar across the organisation, fewer people need to be included at this stage. Although a department store may employ many staff, for example, only a few people from each key job (sales assistant, stockroom controller, supervisor, department manager and store manager, perhaps) need to be included at this stage.

The data collected at this stage must cover the behaviours necessary for effective performance in the jobs to be covered by the competency framework, plus behaviours that will be necessary for effective performance in these jobs, following imminent and expected changes.

Preparing data for analysis

Data-gathering can produce thousands of examples of behaviour. Coding the data will make it easier to manage and will help to check that it represents appropriate sampling within the organisation.

Coding can be set up to show where each behavioural statement came from – eg the job, the function, the job analyst and the job-analysis technique. For example, each statement could be typed up in the following format:

Amends deadlines to account for changes to business priorities.	**Analyst**: Pat Huang **Job title/grade**: Supervisor **Technique**: Interview **Function**: Engineering

By presenting behavioural statements in this way, everybody involved in the data analysis will be able to read behavioural statements collected by other members of the data-gathering team, and know where and how they were collected. Recording all of the data, including its codings, in an electronic spreadsheet or database can also be extremely useful for data analysis.

Coding and classification of the statements should be done as the data-gathering progresses so as to avoid delaying the next step.

Compiling the framework

Once again the three key principles need to be kept in mind throughout this step. Potential users will need to review and help validate initial drafts of the competencies. People need to be kept informed of progress in order to maintain momentum for the project. The main focus of this step is to ensure that the competencies are relevant to the needs of users and intended applications.

There are four key elements to compiling the framework:

- data analysis
- drafting the competency framework
- validation of the draft competencies
- revisions and finalising the competencies.

Data analysis

The primary objective of the data analysis is to organise the data and to ensure that it fully covers the jobs for which the competency framework is intended.

Data analysis and drafting of the competency framework are usually done as one continuous activity. Even for a fairly modest competency framework, two or three days – with lots of space and no distractions – is usually necessary for these stages.

Most team members seem to enjoy the process of collecting the data. The same cannot always be said for the process of analysing the data! Data analysis, to be effective and to prevent it eroding the enthusiasm of the team, needs to be conducted with sufficient time, preparation and structure. It also helps if all individuals involved in the data collection contribute at this stage.

It is important that the structure of the competencies should be allowed to emerge from the data. A structure should not be 'forced' onto the data in the form of preconceived ideas held by the project team. If this does occur, the competencies will simply reflect what the team think or believe should be there, rather than what the data suggests.

In the face of so many behavioural statements, a detailed analysis of all the statements is not practical. An approach which has proved to be very effective is as follows:

- Ensure that behavioural statements collected during the data-gathering stage have been typed up and coded. Separate the statements with their related codings onto individual strips of paper.
- Divide the team into two smaller teams and provide each team with a full set of the statements.
- Each team takes some of their statements (a few handfuls – the rest will be used later) and groups related statements into broad categories, aiming to produce a total of no more than four categories. Typically this is done by taking one statement and placing it on a clear surface. Another statement is selected from the handful of statements and compared with the first statement. If it is considered to be a similar type of behaviour, then it is left with the first statement. If it is considered to be distinctly different it is placed separately from the first. This process is repeated with the remaining handful of statements, combining or dividing grouped statements until there are just three or four piles of statements.

- Each team makes a brief presentation to the other team, describing the broad categories they have produced. The teams identify similarities and differences in the categories and decide which three or four categories will be used for the next step.

- The teams work independently to group *all* of their behavioural statements (including the ones they used in Step 3) into the agreed categories. It is not necessary to dwell long over the meaning of each statement. The teams will be looking at the statements in more detail later.

- Taking each category in turn, each team subdivides its statements (still grouped in categories) into smaller groups of related behaviours. This usually produces three or four groups for each category. These are very rough estimates of the final competencies. A number of refinements may occur during this step, such that groupings are combined or divided as understanding continues to develop about the behaviours within each of the broad categories.

- The teams now reconvene and compare their work. The objective is to work together to agree the basic structure of the competency framework, ie the competency clusters and the competencies. This is achieved by:

  - taking one broad category at a time

  - comparing the groupings of behavioural statements that each team has produced within each category (detailed comparison is not necessary at this stage)

  - agreeing to keep groupings as they are, where they match

  - exploring the reasons where groupings do not match, and subsequently deciding collectively on a revised grouping.

At this stage the clusters and competencies will not be named because changes may still be made to them.

One outcome of this stage may be that gaps are identified in the gathered data – for example no (or very few) behaviours relating to senior-manager roles. If this occurs, the coding should indicate where additional data must be collected. A few cancelled interviews may mean a particular group of jobs has not been included. The team should then collect this data before drafting the framework. A well-planned and monitored project usually avoids this problem.

Drafting the competency framework

Following the last step in the data-analysis stage, the following steps can be used to produce a draft competency framework:

1. The team produces what it considers to be appropriate titles for individual competencies (referred to as 'groupings' in data analysis). The team then moves on to the competency clusters and develops titles for these (referred to as 'categories' in data analysis). This step may be better done in smaller teams, reconvening from time to time to test their ideas and to reach agreements. At this stage it is only necessary to produce brief titles – definitions for competencies and clusters will be developed later.

2. Working now with just one set of behavioural statements, the recombined team reviews the statements under each competency title. The team will decide which behavioural statements should be:

   - moved to another competency because they are now more relevant elsewhere

   - discarded because they are considered too vague to be useful

   - simplified because they are too complicated

   - generalised because they are too specific

   - subdivided because they are considered to contain a number of separate behaviours.

Where statements are rewritten it is important to retain the code(s) from the original statement(s).

3   The team should now eliminate any duplication in the behavioural statements. In this step, all statements which describe the same behaviour are replaced with a single statement. Again, it is important to transfer the codes from the original statements onto the new statement.

4   If levelling is appropriate, the competency levels should be identified directly from the data. A competency framework for which data has been gathered from a number of different job roles may require levelling. Two approaches to levelling are:

- *imposing levels onto the indicators by identifying indicators uniquely relevant to existing job grades.*

    Where data indicates that jobs genuinely require incremental levels of competency consistent with increments in job grade, then, fine: the data is there to prove it. This approach is valid as long as existing job-grade structures are to remain unchanged. If job-grade levels are not going to change, then the coding of the data, which took place during data collection, can be used to identify how a competency differs between job grades – eg how 'teamworking' looks for Grade 2 staff and how it looks different for Grade 3 staff.

- *identifying competency levels direct from the data*

    Within the clustered statements there will be clear indications of different contexts in which the behaviours are important. For example, in 'Decision-making' a number of statements may refer to day-to-day decisions. Other statements may refer to strategic decision-making. These are different competency levels. Using this approach may result in some competencies having only one or two levels while other competencies have several levels.

    There may be a temptation to produce additional levels (by rewriting behavioural statements) if the analysis team feel that there aren't enough levels in a particular competency. It is inappropriate to try to create levels on this basis. It is more rigorous and defensible to identify natural levels within the data – eg based on different contexts and levels of complexity.

There is usually an assumption that competency levels are incremental: that is to say, that behaviours at one level assume that the behaviours at all previous levels are present. The **Appendix Framework** (see page 132) is built on this premise. If this is not the case, there needs to be some indication of it in the framework. Competency frameworks, which include levels that are not incremental, can cause confusion, because each relevant level has to be specified in every role profile created from the framework. For example, a senior role may have all levels in all competencies specified. One way of avoiding independent competency levels is to split the competency. For example, if team leadership does not require team membership behaviours, it may be better to split the behaviours into separate competencies rather than keep them all under one 'teamworking' heading.

These steps will result in the production of a first draft of a competency framework. The draft framework should now be checked to ensure that it conforms to the quality standards listed in the previous chapter. The validation of the draft competencies is part of this checking process.

Validation of the draft competencies
'Validity' here refers to two things:

- Do individuals who demonstrate the competencies perform their work more effectively than colleagues who do not demonstrate the competencies?

- Do individual job-holders recognise the competencies as relevant and necessary for effective performance in their jobs/roles?

The validity of behaviours needed for future needs is established through the processes used to generate these behaviours – provided that appropriate care and expertise were employed at this stage.

Validation of the framework can be undertaken as three distinct tasks:

- feedback on the perceived relevance of the competencies for individual jobs
- feedback on the language used within the framework
- assessment of how well the competencies discriminate between effective and less effective performance.

Feedback on the perceived relevance of competencies for individual jobs can be undertaken using questionnaires or workshops. Job-holders are asked to rate the behaviours within each competency according to how critical they are for achieving their own job objectives. Ratings will help to highlight behaviours that are consistently regarded as irrelevant. However, it is important to remember that individuals may not identify future-oriented behaviours as relevant, so care must be taken when interpreting the results. Alternatively, workshops can be convened to produce competency profiles for the jobs for which the framework has been designed. Difficulties encountered when profiling will help to highlight issues with the comprehensiveness or language used within the competency framework. These activities can also be used to collect feedback on the language used within the framework.

Matching pairs

A major bank was developing a competency framework. In order to validate the first draft, questionnaires were distributed to 250 pairs of staff in six different departments Each pair of staff consisted of a manager and one of their direct reports. Questionnaires contained lists of behavioural indicators from the competencies on which each direct report rated himself or herself in terms of effectiveness. The managers rated their reports using the same form of questionnaire.

Ratings on performance criteria, such as 'achievement of business objectives', were collected for each direct report. Competency ratings were compared with the performance criteria ratings. The data showed that individuals who scored highly on the performance criteria ratings were consistently rated highly on the majority of the competencies.

This demonstrated that the competencies were a valid way of distinguishing between effective and less effective performers.

Assessment of how well the competencies discriminate between effective and less effective performance requires large numbers of job-holders who have been assessed on a single set of performance criteria, eg productivity measures. The same job-holders are then rated on the new competencies – by themselves and their manager. A statistical comparison is then made between the performance measures and the competency ratings. Experts such as occupational psychologists are often used for this work, as results require experience and expertise to interpret.

Revisions and finalising the competencies
Finalising the framework is a matter of fine-tuning based on feedback from the validation stage. As mentioned before, it is necessary to take care when interpreting feedback from the validation stage so

that future-oriented behaviours are not discarded with genuinely irrelevant ones. Care must also be taken when fine-tuning behavioural statements, based on feedback, not to lose the flavour of language used within the organisation.

Once the behavioural indicators and competencies have been refined, definitions can be provided for the competencies and competency levels.

Learning to learn

An FMCG company was introducing new values at the same time as it was finalising a new competency framework. One of the values was about lifelong learning. The draft framework did not fully capture, or represent, this value. So, in fine-tuning the framework prior to launch, some indicators were modified where they contradicted the concept of lifelong learning. For a few competencies new indicators were developed to ensure that the value was fully represented in the framework.

When launching the competency framework, the company communicated how its values had been integrated into the framework. As a result, people using the new competency framework understood why they were being encouraged to adopt a new approach to their development.

Rolling out the framework

Many organisations roll out their frameworks in stages:

- launching the framework
- integrating competencies into processes.

The first stage is a continuation of the key principle of keeping people informed, but it is also necessary to involve the appropriate people – eg it could be key to involve the HR people who will support future users in this stage. The second stage ties together the first and third principles of involving people and ensuring that the competencies are relevant.

It is common for organisations to phase the roll-out – sometimes piloting use of the framework in one part or one level of the organisation – before introducing it to the whole organisation. However, communication about why this is being done should go out to the whole organisation.

If piloting at one level in an organisation it is better to start at the top. This will usually be a small population of senior managers and it sends the right messages to others in the organisation – ie that the competencies are valued and taken seriously at the top.

Launching the framework

This stage is very much about communicating:

- why the framework was produced
- how it was produced
- how it is going to be integrated into the various applications
- how users will be supported in their use of the framework
- how the framework will be kept up to date.

Many of these points will have been made through communications during the preparation, information-gathering and compiling stages. However, these points should be made again in summary to reinforce the fact that so many people have taken part in the process and that it is a business-driven initiative. The roll-out also serves as an opportunity to remind people that the competencies need to be incorporated into people-management processes if they are to be of any use.

All frameworks will need to be kept up to date and it is likely that the more specific the framework, the more frequently it will change – particularly in the language used. All people affected by the framework should understand how they can contribute to keeping it up to date. For example, if representatives are appointed to feed the changes through to a central point, people should be made aware who these representatives are and how to raise issues with them.

Integrating competencies into processes

Launching the framework, and making it available, does not guarantee that the framework will be implemented. Implementation requires users to be trained in the use and interpretation of the competencies, and tools may be needed to assist users further.

It can be very daunting to consider integrating a new competency framework into all people-management processes within the organisation. However, this does not need to be done as a single activity. It is easier to manage and less disruptive if the framework is integrated into processes on a need-to-do basis. If selection is high on the agenda, this may be the place to start. Many organisations conduct performance reviews at a particular time in the year. Preparation for the next round of reviews might include establishing competency profiles and incorporating the competencies into the paperwork.

Ownership of the competency framework will be easier to devolve if line-management users are trained and provided with the tools to do much of this work themselves.

Having been communicated, the process for keeping the framework up to date will need to be implemented as soon as possible.

EXTENDING AN EXISTING FRAMEWORK

A great deal of current competency development is based on extending an existing framework to incorporate a wider range of jobs. When extending a framework, organisations are justifiably reluctant to introduce a whole new set of competencies. In most cases there is no need to introduce a completely new framework, although additional competencies may need to be added to the existing framework.

All the steps and key principles for developing a competency framework from scratch apply when extending a competency framework. The major difference is in the data analysis.

When extending an existing framework to incorporate a wider range of jobs the data analysis can be based on the existing competency structure. Below is a revised version of the data-analysis process for use when extending a competency framework:

- Ensure that behavioural statements collected during the data-gathering stage have been typed up and coded. Separate the statements with their related codings onto individual strips of paper.
- Headings and definitions from the existing competencies are placed on a large work surface. The heading 'Other' must also be placed on the work surface.
- Team members divide up the typed and coded statements and organise them under what they

consider to be the most appropriate existing competencies. Statements that do not fit the existing competencies should be placed under the title 'Other'.

- The competencies are then divided up among pairs of team members who review the statements that have been organised under each of the existing competency headings. Each pair makes a brief presentation to the other team members, giving their views of what they agree and disagree with. During the presentations it may be agreed that some statements should be moved to other competency headings. Relocation of statements should be done at this point. The 'other' pile of statements is left to the next step.

- The team work together to identify whether the 'other' pile of statements represents additional competencies. This can be done by organising the statements into related groups. The approach is similar to analysing data for a competency framework being built from scratch – eg by taking one statement and placing it on a clear surface. Another statement is selected from the remaining statements and compared with the first statement. If it is considered to be a similar type of behaviour, it is left with the first statement. If it is considered to be distinctly different, it is placed separately from the first. This process is repeated with the remaining statements, combining or dividing grouped statements until they represent groups of competency-level statements.

If any gaps are identified in the gathered data – eg data missing from particular jobs – then this will need to be supplemented by obtaining appropriate additional data.

The team then draft the new competency framework using steps 2, 3 and 4 of the process used for drafting a competency framework when developing a framework from scratch. (Step 1 is not required because the competency structure already exists.) The remaining activities for compiling a competency framework and for rolling out a competency framework are the same as those for developing a competency framework from scratch.

UPDATING A FRAMEWORK

All competency frameworks will require updating at some stage. The need for updating may be small – eg a minor change in working conditions – or substantial – eg a major change in the way the organisation operates. In either case, some form of monitoring is needed to identify change factors likely to influence the way individuals undertake their work. Small changes will usually be easy to accommodate and may simply require amending a few behaviours or adding a few new behaviours. Significant changes may have an impact on the whole framework

Once a change factor has been identified the next task is to identify its effect on the behaviours required to carry out job demands. We have found structured workshops with a mix of specialists and job-holders to be particularly helpful for this task. The workshops are structured around the change factor(s), and for each competency the question is asked, 'What will people need to do differently because of this factor?' Techniques such as force-field analysis and focused questioning are used to expand this question and to identify whether additional competencies are required. These techniques will also help identify whether any existing competencies are redundant because of the changes.

In most cases changes can be made directly to the existing competencies. In some cases the workshops may indicate that updating isn't sufficient and a new framework needs to be developed. In all cases, appropriate people need to be involved and communication about why changes are being made is essential. Finally, close monitoring of the updated framework is needed to ensure that, when the anticipated change occurs, the changed competencies adequately reflect the new behaviours required.

DEVELOPING A SPECIFIC FRAMEWORK FROM SCRATCH

There are occasions when a framework is required for a specific need. This need may be for recruiting into a particular group of jobs or to address particular issues within an organisation. We have worked with organisations that were not interested in complete, organisation-wide competencies, as they felt they only needed competencies to help address particular issues: for example, developing a set of leadership competencies for one organisation or a set of people-management competencies for another. However, be wary of producing several specific frameworks for use within one organisation. Having several specific frameworks in use in one organisation is likely to create confusion, and it loses out on the benefits that generic frameworks bring – eg helping individuals to see how development in one role can prepare them for succession to another role, and providing a common language to describe effective performance across the organisation.

The steps that need to be undertaken to produce a specific framework are the same as those described for developing a competency framework from scratch, but on a smaller scale. The main areas of difference are in:

- data collection
- data analysis
- drafting of the framework.

All previous comments regarding principles and techniques for data collection still apply. The main difference is that data collection can focus much more closely on job- or application-specific examples of behaviours. For example, an issue-based framework such as leadership can focus on the behaviours observed when leadership activities are carried out. A specific framework for a narrow range of administrative roles could include behavioural statements that refer to specific processes and procedures used in those roles. In addition, the sample of job-holders from which to gather information will be smaller than that for a generic framework. However, it is important to ensure that the sample is large enough to pick up important differences between the jobs or activities for which the framework is being developed. Depending on the number of similar jobs to be covered by the framework, preparing data for analysis – ie coding the data – can usually be simplified where less coding information is needed.

The analysis stage will usually involve fewer behavioural statements than the same stage when producing a generic framework. However, the same steps can be applied to the statements. The main difference here is that the more detailed behavioural statements should make sorting of the data easier, because it is easier to classify specific behaviours.

When drafting the competency framework, a key consideration should be to ensure that rewording of behavioural statements does not result in the statements losing their specific focus.

As with the production of a generic framework, the people who produce a specific framework need to be trained and skilled in the use of data-gathering and data-analysis techniques.

Rolling out a specific framework is also easier, as its scope is much narrower than that of a generic framework. Provided the key principles have been followed during the development of the framework, even the roll-out of a framework to address performance issues such as leadership or people management can be straightforward.

ADAPTING AN EXISTING FRAMEWORK TO MEET SPECIFIC NEEDS

Generic competency frameworks – ie frameworks that apply across all or most of an organisation – can often be used without adaptation for general applications, such as discussing general performance. For situations that require accuracy, such as selection or reviewing an individual's performance in a particular job, generic behavioural indicators will need to be made situation-specific.

To adapt generic behaviours to specific situations typically means making the behavioural indicators more precise. Behavioural indicators are needed that provide clear and detailed examples of what each competency looks like when observed in a particular job or role. Ideal people to supply this detail are job experts, such as existing job-holders and their managers. For each generic behavioural indicator these experts need to answer the question 'What would I see if I were observing an effective person employing this behaviour in this job?' Answering this question can produce more than one example. Therefore, it is not uncommon to have three behaviours for a competency level in a generic framework and six or seven behavioural examples used for that same competency level in an assessment.

Detailed indicators can be developed using:

- an interview
- a facilitated group approach
- questionnaires.

It is important that each detailed indicator is both relevant to the competency level and the job, and that it conforms to the standards for indicators described in Chapter 2 (**A Typical Competency Framework**).

Although behaviours need to be job-specific, in some situations – eg when used for assessing external candidates to fill job vacancies – they must not be so specific that they could be demonstrated only by someone who is already doing the job. Behaviours must be worded in a way which ensures that they will not exclude individuals who have demonstrated similar behaviours in other situations. For example, although 'Checks sales figures for electric toasters with inventory' is an example of 'Establishes accuracy of information', it is too specific for use in selection. Using this specific example excludes anyone who hasn't worked in sales or with electric toasters.

Further guidance on adapting competencies to specific applications is provided in the particular applications chapters.

KEY POINTS

- Producing a competency framework that meets the needs of a wide range of users requires a structured approach.
- There are three key principles that must be followed when developing a competency framework:
    - Key principle 1 – involve the people who will be affected by the framework.
    - Key principle 2 – keep people informed about what is happening and why.
    - Key principle 3 – create competencies that are relevant to all those who will be affected by them as well as to organisational needs and intended applications.
- In most cases competency frameworks are developed from scratch or extended from an existing framework.
- All frameworks should be reviewed and updated as necessary and, in some cases, competency frameworks will need to be developed or adapted for specific needs.

- A four-step process has been identified for developing competencies, and each of these can be broken down into important subactivities:

- Preparation
  - getting buy-in from key people
  - clarification of purpose
  - planning the project
  - putting a data-gathering/analysis team together.

- Collecting information
  - choosing analysis techniques
  - data-gathering
  - preparing data for analysis.

- Compiling the framework
  - data analysis
  - drafting the competency framework
  - validation of the draft competencies
  - revising and finalising the competencies.

- Rolling out the framework
  - launching the framework
  - integrating competencies into processes.

- The production of a competency framework is a process which combines views of what happens within jobs or roles with visions of the future.

- The techniques required to gather the necessary data must be applied with discipline and skill to ensure that the data collected is as objective as possible.

- Where possible all who will be affected by the framework should have contributed to its production at some stage. If the organisation is too large to include all people, then those who are included must be recognised as truly representative by everyone who will be affected by the framework.

- The definitions and structure of the competency framework are dictated by the data itself. Imposing pre-set structures or ideas onto the data when there is no evidence to support them undermines the rigour and effort invested in collecting the data.

- Relevance of the competency framework should be evident to its users in the language used, but it should also be tested and proven before the framework is implemented.

- Once the framework is launched, users must be provided with the necessary support, training and tools to implement the framework.

- A process should be implemented for keeping the framework relevant and up to date.

REFERENCES AND READING

GHORPADE, J. V. (1988) *Job Analysis: A handbook for human resource directors*. New Jersey, Prentice-Hall.

PEARN, M. A. and KANDOLA, R. S. (1993) *Job Analysis: A manager's guide*. 2nd edition. London, Institute of Personnel Management.

Using competencies in selection

Use of the term 'competency-based selection' overemphasises the importance of competencies and diverts attention away from other critical factors. Selection processes have drifted towards a primary focus on competencies. Indeed, many sophisticated selection processes, including assessment centres, now assess only competencies. Yet a thorough assessment of performance must at least take account of how well an individual completes work-relevant activities as well as how he or she goes about those activities.

For many organisations, improved selection will be achieved if greater attention is given to using selection exercises and processes that are better matched to the job vacancy and by investing more time and effort into the training of assessors. Of course, appropriate selection criteria are crucial and a good competency framework will help in this area as well as in helping to set up and design selection processes.

THE PURPOSE OF SELECTION

We use 'selection' here to refer to all processes in which individuals are attracted to and assessed for placement into roles within an organisation, whether the applicants are internal or external to the organisation, permanent or temporary. The primary purpose of selection is to place individuals who can make effective and worthwhile contributions to an organisation into appropriate jobs or roles. We use the term 'applicant' to cover individuals at the application and sifting stage, and the term 'candidate' for those who pass from the application stage into the assessment and decision-making stages.

Some organisations have made use of competency-based assessment to select individuals for redundancy – more accurately referred to as deselection. If individuals are being deselected from existing job roles then selection-type assessments should not be necessary. An effective performance management process should identify and manage individuals who are not providing effective contributions through their work. If jobs are changing so significantly that existing employees have to be assessed for the newly formed jobs, then the assessment process is likely to resemble a selection process for external applicants.

EFFECTIVE SELECTION PROCESSES

Effective selection processes have a number of elements:

- selection criteria
- assessment methods
- decision rules.

Each of these elements must be relevant to the specific vacancy (usually referred to as validity) and must be capable of being applied consistently to achieve consistent results (usually referred to as reliability).

Competencies alone are insufficient to make effective use of these elements. To illustrate this we have compared selection with the processes used when buying a car. While we are not suggesting that people are like cars, we are saying that *processes* undertaken when buying a car (or, indeed, making any major purchase) are similar to the *processes* used when selecting people.

Buying a car

A buyer needs to decide what to look for in a car (the selection criteria); he or she must decide how to assess specific cars (the assessment methods) and then decide which one best suits his or her needs (the decision rules). Selection criteria the car buyer will use may include:

- appearance – eg colour, state of bodywork
- safety features
- history and mileage
- engine size
- model – eg saloon, hatchback, convertible
- number of seats
- performance
- price.

Assessment methods the car buyer will use may include:

- looking at its general appearance
- using a checklist of essential characteristics
- asking how good the owner thinks the car is
- questioning previous owners on the history of the car
- looking at the handbook and service history
- asking for specific examples of the car's performance
- taking it for a test-drive
- making predictions based on technical characteristics of the car.

The car buyer may undertake more than one of the above assessments before making a decision on whether to purchase the car or not. Some assessments will not provide the best measure of a car's suitability. For example, buying a car because it looks OK and the owner says it is a great car to drive is at best going to leave the car buyer unprepared for what is wrong with the car, and at worst leave him or her having made a very expensive mistake.

Short of taking the car away for a few months to try it out, a test-drive is probably the most accurate means of assessing its suitability. It enables the car to be driven in realistic situations while undertaking tasks that represent the everyday operations the car will be required to perform. For example, if the car is to be used for long motorway journeys with a full load as well as for trips around town, then ideally these conditions should be part of the test-drive.

There are some assessments that a buyer may wish to make before he or she undertakes a test-drive. These assessments will prevent the buyer from viewing a car which does not meet certain basic requirements. For example, he or she may wish to check that the car has a certain number of seats because, however suitable the car is in other ways, without the right minimum number of seats there would be no point in viewing it.

There are also some assessments the car buyer may wish to make after taking it for a test-drive. These will relate to areas that won't be covered by driving the car. For example, the car buyer may wish to check the car's ownership, maintenance and service history – the car may perform well in the test-drive, but the maintenance and service history may indicate the car to be unreliable or costly to maintain.

With all this information the car buyer needs to be consistent in the way that information for each car is then compared before arriving at his or her final decision.

The use of criteria describing how the car should perform given certain conditions and then testing the car against these criteria through a test-drive would come closest to a purely competency-based selection process. These 'competencies' might include 'operates efficiently whilst fully loaded', 'conveys drivers and passengers comfortably over long distances' and so on.

The car buyer illustration shows that a thorough process for selecting one car from many contenders requires the buyer to collect a wide range of different information using different methods of assessment. For example, a simple test-drive is unlikely to assess all of the vehicle's safety features. Accurate assessment depends on a thorough understanding and consistent application of *all* the appropriate assessment criteria.

The car buyer also needs to use an appropriate process and appropriate skills to make reliable and relevant comparisons between each tested vehicle in order to select the vehicle that at least meets the minimum acceptable standard on each appropriate criterion.

This chapter deals with best-practice in selection when using competencies. In reality, there are times when it may be tempting to short-cut the selection process. For example, a vacancy requires filling urgently. Continuing with the car theme, this is akin to needing to replace a car quickly. It may be tempting to buy the first car available for sale, but this can turn out to be an expensive mistake. For example, having bought it, the car buyer may realise that he or she hadn't thought through what was needed or, by rushing their decision, didn't test the car properly, and it turns out to need a lot of expensive maintenance. It may have been more cost-effective to hire a car or use taxis to allow time to establish the type of car needed and to find the right car through appropriate testing. Likewise, with the urgently needed new recruit, it may be tempting to short-cut the recruitment process and take an educated guess at selection criteria or rush through the selection decision. However, using an agency or temporary worker may provide the necessary time to establish exactly what is needed to permanently fill the vacancy. The chances of making a bad selection decision increase with every compromise made in selection. As organisations have to take on the responsibilities and costs of managing the outcome of a selection decision, it needs to be the best one possible.

USING COMPETENCIES IN SELECTION

Effective selection requires skilled selectors to assess applicants, using relevant assessment criteria (not just competencies) and relevant assessment methods before taking decisions about the suitability of applicants for a particular vacancy. Competencies alone are not sufficient to ensure an effective selection process, but they can be used in selection:

- as selection criteria
- to attract and sift applicants
- to assess candidates
- as benchmarks for decision-making
- for giving assessment feedback
- as criteria for monitoring the selection process.

Using competencies as selection criteria

The term 'competency-based selection' can be misleading, for effective selection will always include other assessment criteria.

Selection is not just about assessing potential job performance. Other factors may restrict individuals from being employed for specific jobs – for example:

- legal requirements to hold a particular qualification: eg heavy goods vehicle (HGV) licence-holder for a driver of HGVs
- minimum legal working age
- ability to spend time away from home – eg long-haul pilot.

Different types and stages of assessment use or seek information in addition to that which can be provided using competencies. See, for example, Table 5.

Table 5 *Additional information required by various forms of assessment*

Type of assessment	Additional information
References	previous history, perceptions of others
Screening criteria/CV	previous experience, qualifications, personal circumstances
Interview	previous experience, knowledge, attitudes, aspirations
Work sample or simulation	job tasks, job context, performance standards
Tests/questionnaires	ability, personality, motivation

'Competencies are behaviours that individuals demonstrate when undertaking job-relevant tasks effectively within a given organisational context' (our definition from Chapter 1 – **What Do We Mean by 'Competencies'?**). Competencies are therefore best assessed when potential job-holders are observed while undertaking job-relevant tasks in a realistic and appropriate organisational environment.

There are three things that can be done to improve the contribution competencies make as selection criteria:

1 Identify the competencies or competency levels which are *critical* for effective performance in the job. This will minimise the total number of competencies to be assessed in selection. Six to eight critical/essential competencies are usually sufficient.

2 Identify competencies that might be used to distinguish between applicants who are equally suitable on the critical competencies. These are 'desirable competencies', and although not critical they must be important for performance in the job.

3 Identify detailed examples of the generic behavioural indicators – ie what these generic behaviours look like in the target job.

Identify recruitment-critical competencies

There is usually a trade-off between assessment of every possible factor that can affect performance and the resources (eg time, money and people) available for selection. Restricting competency assessments to competencies that are critical for performance at the required level reduces the time and effort needed to develop and manage selection without seriously undermining the process. By limiting the number of competencies, the recruitment process also avoids trying to make all job-holders the same. By using only those competencies that are essential to the job there are still many ways in which job-holders will differ.

Here is an approach for identifying 'recruitment-critical' competencies for a job or role:

- List the most critical job tasks required to meet the job purpose.
- List the competencies that would be essential to carry out each of these tasks effectively.

- If the framework includes levels, identify them in the same way.
- Establish whether individuals could develop sufficiently quickly to an acceptable level in any of the listed competencies once in the job. If so, these competencies could be left out of the selection process.
- The remaining competencies are the essential ones.

These steps can be undertaken together with existing job-holders and/or their managers because these individuals should have the most realistic view of the job. Involvement also enhances buy-in to the resulting criteria and selection decisions.

A similar approach can be used for new jobs, or jobs undergoing significant change, provided that the key tasks and responsibilities have been identified for the new job. In these situations, individuals with knowledge of the demands of the tasks and responsibilities of the new job can be used to help identify recruitment-critical competencies. These individuals may have experience of components of the new job – that is, they may currently or previously have undertaken or managed some of the tasks or responsibilities. In many cases a group of people who have experience of different components of the new job can, between them, provide a sufficient view of the whole job.

Identify desirable competencies
It can happen that, using essential criteria, several candidates appear equally suited for a vacancy. In this case further selection criteria (eg desirable competencies) can be used to help shortlist. Desirable competencies can be produced by identifying competencies that would enhance performance in the job. Identifying these desirable competencies also helps to check that critical competencies really are critical.

Make-your-mind-up time

A major financial institution was running a number of assessment centres to recruit in to a team leader role. When designing the selection process, 'influencing' was deemed to be critical. It was decided that if a candidate achieved an unacceptable score on any critical competency the candidate would be rejected.

One candidate on the assessment centre was rated high or acceptable on all competencies except 'influencing', in which his score was 'unacceptable'. The managers conducting the assessments agreed that the candidate had demonstrated that he could do the job despite being rated unacceptable on influencing. The managers decided to override the original rules of the assessment centre, saying that influencing was important but not critical for performance in the job.

In the above example, a competency previously thought critical actually was not. Managers involved in the design of this assessment centre should have asked themselves this question – a challenge for all critical criteria:

 If an applicant achieved an unacceptable score on this selection criterion but highly on every other one, would we still wish to progress his or her application?

If the answer is 'yes', then that criterion is not a critical one.

Competencies identified as important but not critical – ie they would enhance job performance but without them job performance would still be acceptable – can be included in the later stages of selection to help where there are too many candidates who make the grade on critical competencies.

In order to keep the assessment process reliable, it is important that all selection criteria, essential and desirable, are decided before the selection process starts.

Identify detailed examples of behavioural indicators

Where assessment criteria are written in general terms, as in generic competencies, the criteria could be subject to different interpretations – eg where assessors have little or no detailed knowledge of the vacancy. In selection this can reduce the reliability and validity of selection decisions. Therefore, in addition to identifying 'recruitment-critical' competencies/levels, it can be useful to produce detailed examples of the relevant behavioural indicators.

Detailed examples of behavioural indicators will be needed when using a generic competency framework (refer to the ' Adapting an existing framework to meet specific needs' section in Chapter 3 – **Developing a Competency Framework**) and/or when assessment exercises are being designed for specific vacancies (refer to the 'Designing simulations for specific vacancies' section later in this chapter).

Using competencies to attract and sift applicants

Having established *all* appropriate criteria for the job vacancy and ensured that they are valid, the next step is to attract appropriate applicants and ensure that only those with a reasonable chance of matching the job requirements are then passed through to the assessment stage. Many organisations could make better use of competencies to inform potential applicants about a vacancy.

Criteria such as qualifications and experience typically feature more at this early stage of selection. Competencies – although useful and becoming more common at this stage – are often more prominent later in the selection process. Criteria that would restrict or bar applicants from doing the job should be reviewed first – eg a requirement to work overseas or a legal requirement to hold a professional or technical qualification. If applicants pass these requirements, competency information can be used to sift out individuals who would make poor candidates at the assessment stage.

The rating and scoring of application forms is addressed later in this chapter in the 'Using competencies to make sift and selection decisions' section.

Attracting applicants

Advertisements should aim to attract better-suited applicants while dissuading unsuitable applicants.

More and more job advertisements now include competency information as a way of indicating the type of person the organisation is keen to attract. Just as generic behavioural indicators can lead to inconsistency in assessments, general competency information in advertisements – such as competency headings or generic behavioural indicators – can lead to inconsistency in the suitability of applicants.

Organisations need to communicate the details of vacancies to relevant audiences. The communication – most likely to be an advertisement of some description – has to contain enough information to attract the right applicants.

Compare the following two approaches:

> *This role requires people with a proven track record of: working with people; working with information; developing the business; achieving results.*

> *Successful Customer Services staff operate as part of a team, providing support to each other and sharing experiences. The role is demanding and it is important that you are able to adapt your style to the different styles of others and to present information in different ways when customers don't understand you the first time. Written and spoken information feature a lot in the work and it is important that you can quickly spot the information that is important and where to find it.*

The first example says very little about what is required of potential job-holders. Many jobs could be described using these competencies, and many applicants could therefore decide they have the necessary experience to make it worth their while applying for the job. This type of advertisement can result in a high proportion of inappropriate applicants.

The second example restricts the range of competency information to those competencies which are most critical while providing examples of why the competencies are important. These examples are taken from the behavioural indicators and demonstrate the importance of using everyday language in competencies. The wording in Example 2 is much more likely to help applicants to decide whether or not the vacancy matches their skills and experience, and therefore increases the proportion of relevant applicants.

Sifting applicants

Information required to assess applicants for early sifting in a selection process is usually collected using an application form.

It is important to consider whether communication of the type required to complete the application form is relevant in the job. For example, not all jobs require good written English. There may be applicants who have the competencies required to do a job, but who have difficulty with reading and writing. If the application form is used to screen out these applicants, they will not have another opportunity to demonstrate their competencies and will have been treated unfairly. Where reading or written communication is not required in the job, alternatives to application forms should be considered. Recruitment-critical competencies should provide a clear indication of the relevance of a written application form for a specific vacancy.

Other methods of collecting applicant information for early sifting include:

- telephone-based questionnaires, by which applicants are asked questions and for which they use the keypad to provide answers or speak their responses
- questionnaires administered via computer, either on a disk or through the Internet.

Whatever the form of collecting applicant information and sifting, the process qualifies as an assessment method. As with any assessment method, it should be tested to ensure that it consistently produces relevant information for making appropriate sifting decisions.

In addition to general applicant details and information on essential criteria, such as necessary qualifications, these methods now often include a section for collecting competency information.

Competency information can be collected in several ways:

- open-format questionnaires
- a competency-rating questionnaires
- a forced-choice questionnaires.

Open-format questionnaires

The open-format approach is best suited to written application forms and requires applicants to provide one or two examples of how the applicant has used each job-critical competency.

Open-format approaches have two main drawbacks. Firstly, applicants do not always provide the types of examples needed to make a fair sifting decision, and marking these questionnaires can be very time-consuming. Secondly, open-format questionnaires can suffer from 'rater bias'. Rater bias can occur when raters have difficulty reading or interpreting applicants' responses.

While rater bias can be dealt with through careful training, the first difficulty – applicants providing inappropriate examples – is almost impossible to eliminate. In addition, applicants often comment that they do not like this style of questionnaire. Difficulties in producing reliable sifting decisions from open-format questionnaires have encouraged organisations to use the more structured-type competency questionnaires described below.

Where open-format questionnaires are used, guidance needs to be given to applicants on each competency. For example, to collect information on 'Developing others' an application form might include the following (with enough space for the applicant to write an answer!):

> This job involves developing others. In the space below, please provide two examples of where you have had to manage the development of others. Please ensure that you indicate the issues you dealt with, how you dealt with them and the results.

Alternatively, applicants can be given more of a lead by providing specific questions to answer within each competency. For example:

DEVELOPING OTHERS

Provide two examples of where you have had to manage the development of others.

What issues did you have to deal with?

What did you do?

What were the outcomes?

These example 'prompts' are based on generic competency behaviours. At this stage, and with the limited information that can be collected in an application form, it is often appropriate to use competencies at this level of detail. However, for jobs that require a high degree of experience closely

Table 6 *Competency-rating questionnaire*

Rate how often you do the following: (Key: 1 = usually, 2 = often, 3 = rarely, 4 = never.)				
a. account for the impact of your decisions on others				
b. share your learning experiences with colleagues				
c. talk about the achievements of your employer outside of work				
d. identify and seek out information you think you need for your job				
e. etc.				

matched to the vacancy, it would be better to use the more detailed versions of behaviours described earlier.

Competency-rating questionnaires

Competency-rating questionnaires require applicants to rate themselves on statements taken from the behavioural indicators listed within the competency. Behaviours may be rated on a scale to indicate how frequently the applicant uses the behaviour effectively. See, for example, Table 6. This example has taken behaviours from several competencies and converted them into questionnaire statements.

Just listing behaviours from the competencies will not produce an effective questionnaire because most applicants will soon realise that they can present a good image by rating each statement as a '1' or a '2'. It is usual, in questionnaires of this type, to reverse half of the statements so that applicants are required to rate some statements as '3' or '4' to indicate suitability for the vacancy. For example, 'talk about the achievements of your employer outside work' might become 'underplay or avoid talking about achievements of your employer outside work'. This type of questionnaire must be carefully designed and worded so that the behaviours desired by the organisation are not obvious. This must be achieved without making the questionnaire unnecessarily difficult to complete.

Forced-choice questionnaires

The forced-choice questionnaire presents applicants with pairs of statements. It is intended that the applicant will believe all statements to be equally desirable from the viewpoint of the recruiting organisation. However, each pair of statements contains a behaviour that is desirable to the organisation and a behaviour that is undesirable to the organisation – each from a different competency. 'Undesirable' behaviours must be relevant to the recruitment-critical competencies so that applicants selecting the behaviours will still be providing information relevant to the vacancy. See the example below.

From each pair of statements choose the statement that describes you better.

a. Adapts personal style to develop relationships.
b. Complete own tasks before helping colleagues.

c. Presents own views with conviction.
d. Moves people on from mistakes by focusing on what went well.

e. When encountering blocks to progress, quickly moves to other, more achievable tasks.
f. Seeks and gives constructive feedback.

g. etc
h. etc

As with the competency-rating approach, this questionnaire is based on behaviours from the recruitment-critical competencies. In the above example the **Appendix Framework** has been used to develop three of the statements. Statements *b*, *d* and *e* are negative examples of behaviours from 'GROWS INDIVIDUAL CAPABILITY: Developing, Level 3' (page 134).

- provides support and feedback to colleagues when needed
- helps people to learn from mistakes
- identifies and removes or works around blocks to progress, as appropriate.

Using competencies to assess candidates

Any method of assessment used in selection should provide results that are:

- reliable – ie produces consistent results
- valid – ie provides appropriate measurement of relevant criteria.

Whilst selection is likely to include assessment of many types of criteria, our concern in this book is to ensure that assessment of competencies is made in a reliable and valid way.

Where a large number of job-holders occupy positions for which the selection process is being designed, all assessment methods, including application forms and interviews, should be statistically tested against job performance criteria.

Reliability can be tested by comparing the results of tests administered to a particular group with scores obtained from the same group on the same tests at another point in time under the same conditions.

Validity of assessment methods can be tested by using the following process:

1 Use the assessment methods with existing job-holders.
2 Collect ratings of job performance for each job-holder. Where possible, collect 'hard' measures of performance such as targets completed or sales achieved. (Note: at least 50, ideally 100 or more, job-holders are required to complete each assessment method and provide performance ratings.)
3 Scores obtained from the assessment methods are then compared with job performance scores.

The most common statistical analysis used when comparing these types of data is referred to as a test of 'correlation'. Results from this form of analysis are frequently used to report the relationship between assessment methods and job performance – ie how well scores on assessment methods predict scores on job performance. It is often suggested that an assessment method that correlates 0.3 or above with job performance is a useful method. However, there is more to correlation than a single number, and it is meaningless to say 0.3 is good or bad.

The descriptions provided above for testing reliability and validity are very much simplified. We do not cover the subject of statistical analysis of data in this book. We do recommend, though, that anyone in a position to undertake statistical testing of assessment methods should ensure that it is done, and that they have access to expertise in statistical analysis.

The vast majority of selection programmes have insufficient numbers of applicants or existing job-holders for statistical analysis to be meaningful. However, well-designed assessment methods based on competencies, job tasks and job outputs can ensure sufficient correspondence between the assessment methods and the job to provide confidence in their validity (refer to the 'Designing simulations for specific vacancies' section, page 63). If using off-the-shelf assessment exercises where there are few existing job-holders, the validity of an exercise can be estimated by:

- comparing tasks and required outputs in the assessment exercise with tasks and required outputs in the job, to ensure that the exercise reflects the job
- ensuring that evidence collected when using these exercises with a sample of existing job-holders includes sufficient relevant examples of the competencies which the exercise is intended to measure.

There are a number of different ways in which candidates can be assessed:

- interviews
- off-the-shelf tests and questionnaires (psychometrics)
- work sample tests
- simulations
- assessment centres for selection.

Interviews

Interviews work well when they:

- are structured
- employ clear and relevant criteria
- are used by well-trained, skilful and disciplined interviewers.

Interviewers find it easier to stay focused on the appropriate competencies when they use an interviewing guide. This contains guidelines for conducting an interview, such as a structure to follow and information to include in the introduction, along with a clear guide to the questions that might be asked for each competency. The interviewer's skill is used to ensure that sufficient information is collected for all of the competencies included in the interview.

A competency-based interview will seek evidence that the interviewee has employed behaviours like those listed in the competencies. A good interviewer will aim to elicit examples of what has been achieved with the behaviours (eg successful outcomes). The good interviewer will also seek to ensure that the interviewee has used the behaviours in appropriate situations – ie that the successes were relevant to a level similar to that of the vacancy.

Competency-based interviews can be as good or as poor as the best or worst interviews.

Oral questionnaires?

A major bank used competency-based interviewing as part of its selection process for customer service staff. More than a hundred staff were recruited using the interview as part of the process. Only accredited interviewers, trained in a very disciplined approach to interviewing, were used to conduct interviews.

Assessment records indicated that very little evidence had actually been collected regarding the competencies during any of the interviews. Further analysis showed that decisions to select or reject a candidate were not based on any of the competencies.

Interviewers had been misguided in how to structure their questions – the process itself did not allow an interviewer the necessary freedom to keep the interview focused on the competencies. In fact, most interviewers were simply reading out each question and noting the reply: no probing or supplementary questions were being asked.

The interview was focused on the right competencies but the supporting materials and training were getting in the way. Retraining and new interview guidelines provided a quick, but necessary, remedy.

Although competencies can contribute to an excellent interview, this example shows that, on their own, they cannot guarantee one.

Apart from the opening and the closing sections of the competency-based interview, the majority of the time requires the interviewee to provide examples of previous performance. Interviewers focus the responses of interviewees using questions drawn directly from the competencies. The competencies explored in an interview should be compatible with the interview process. For example, as the interview collects evidence only of reported performance, it is not suitable for collecting actual evidence of problem-solving. Problems tackled by the interviewees and their knowledge of problem-solving techniques could be explored during the interview, but assessment exercises which actually test this competency are likely to be more informative.

An example of questions that might be asked in a competency-based interview is given below:

Shows the way: Direction

Level 2: Keeps others informed of business goals and inspires buy-in to them

Have you been in situations where you had to inspire others to buy-in to business goals ?

Describe one such situation to me.

What was your role?

Describe what you did to inspire buy-in.

What was the outcome?

What contribution did others make to the outcome?

An experienced interviewer would not necessarily ask all, or only, these questions and might reword them to complement the responses of the interviewee. Competency-based interview schedules are not scripts to be followed slavishly – they are guidelines to ensure consistency. They provide an agenda or checklist for collecting appropriate examples of competency. Nevertheless, good competency-based interviews have a clear and noticeable structure.

Off-the-shelf tests and questionnaires (psychometrics)

'Off-the-shelf' ability tests and personality questionnaires are frequently used in selection and are often referred to as psychometric tests. These are highly standardised tests which must be administered under very strict conditions. The term 'test' usually applies to measures of specific abilities, but this category is often taken to include measures of personality and motivation.

Off-the-shelf psychometric tests and questionnaires are not direct measures of competencies. In Chapter 1 (**What Do We Mean by 'Competencies'?**), it was shown that characteristics of a person – such as abilities and personality – influence the way the person behaves. Psychometric tests measure some of the characteristics that can influence behaviour – they do not measure how a person behaves when using these characteristics.

In the car analogy used earlier, tests would tell us about specific characteristics of the car. A garage might, for example, test the power and functioning of a car's brakes, engine and steering. Because these characteristics are important for a car's overall performance, the test results would provide valid information on which to decide – whether or not to proceed with further assessment. For example, if the car fails on these tests it is unlikely that a potential buyer would want to continue their assessment and test the vehicle at speed on a motorway. However, a car may pass the above tests, but may behave very poorly when fully loaded at motorway speeds.

Relevant tests might predict aspects of performance, but they do not provide evidence of actual behaviour in specific situations. If these types of test are to be used in competency-based assessments, it is vital that tests are chosen that will help to screen out individuals who lack *characteristics essential* for performance in the job.

When tests count!

A major bank was recruiting graduates for work in foreign exchange roles. The roles laid considerable dependence on numerical skills. An assessment centre had been designed to assess competencies. There were more than 600 applicants for the roles. Sifting by application forms reduced this number to 150. An ability test was designed to measure job-relevant numerical ability and used to further sift applicants down to manageable numbers for the assessment centres.

All candidates attending the assessment centres were able to deal with numerical aspects of the job-simulation exercises. Thus time was not wasted using elaborate assessment centres to measure the competencies of individuals lacking basic skills.

Work sample tests

Another type of ability test with psychometric properties is the 'work sample' test. Such tests are usually designed for a particular recruitment campaign and focus on job-specific activities and can also focus on job-specific competencies. The results from these tests can usually be integrated with other competency assessments, especially when the design is based around the specific competencies relevant to the vacancy.

Testing, testing

A government agency wished to recruit a large number of counter staff. The role involved a great deal of form-filling and checking of forms completed by others. Competencies for these roles included 'attention to detail' and 'following instructions'.

Two tests were devised. The first test involved completing two forms using instructions provided within the test. The second test involved examining different forms that had already been completed in order to identify any errors.

Because there were over 100 existing counter staff, the tests were checked by examining how good performers in the job scored on the tests and how poorer job performers scored. Test scores showed that good job performers scored significantly higher on the tests than poorer performers. The tests were adopted as measures of 'attention to detail' and 'following instructions' and used in the selection process.

Work sample tests do not just copy job tasks. Care is required in the design of these tests and expertise is required to establish rules for scoring. For these reasons, work sample tests are usually developed by experts in psychometric test design.

Simulations

Short of taking applicants on for a few months to 'try them out', a series of work-related exercises will usually provide the most accurate assessment of an applicant's competency suitability. This approach enables applicants to be assessed in realistic situations while undertaking tasks that represent the everyday tasks that the job-holder would be required to perform to produce job-relevant outputs.

Simulations may sound similar to work sample tests, but they differ in important ways. These are illustrated in Table 7.

Table 7 *The differences between work samples and simulations*

Work sample	Simulation
Based on a single task – eg filling in a form	Based on one or more objectives – eg resolving team issues
Assesses one competency	Assesses several competencies
Psychometric – ie standardised measure of personal characteristics	Not usually psychometric
Usually multiple-choice answers or defined range of acceptable answers	Answers not predefined – behavioural indicators used for assessing answers
Task is highly constrained	Objectives are broadly defined
An overall score is calculated for the test	A rating is assigned to each competency

Commonly used simulations include:

- in-tray (in-basket) exercises
- group discussions
- role plays
- case studies
- presentations.

Ideally, simulations will be developed, based on the job for which individuals are being assessed. In part this is because simulations provide an opportunity to 'test-drive' candidates.

As simulations are more resource-hungry than other assessment exercises (eg increased assessor time), most organisations sift applicants in terms of their general suitability for the vacancy before inviting them for simulation-based assessments.

Although vacancy-specific simulations would provide the best 'test-drive', many organisations use off-the-shelf simulations. These are an inevitable compromise between cost/time and quality of assessment. Off-the-shelf simulations can only approximate to an organisation's job activities, required outputs and competencies.

Research has shown that certain types of simulations are better at providing evidence on some competencies than on others. This sort of research makes the choice of simulations easier, but it can also mislead recruiters into believing that the specific off-the-shelf simulation(s) they purchase will be suited to their vacancy and their competencies. The research should be used only as a guide.

Every assessment exercise should be evaluated to ensure that it provides job-relevant opportunities for candidates to demonstrate the behaviours contained in the recruitment-critical competencies. To ensure this relevance with off-the-shelf simulations it will usually be necessary, at least, to:

- customise instructions for candidates
- rewrite guidelines for assessors
- amend the scoring system.

To ensure that simulations provide a comprehensive and reliable assessment of all recruitment-critical competencies it is normal to use several simulations in a single assessment. A grid of competencies and simulations that could be used to test them is usually produced, in which:

- Each competency is measured at least twice.
- Poor performance on one competency does not make it difficult to demonstrate effective performance on other competencies within the same simulation. For example, 'objective-setting' and 'planning' should not be assessed together, because agreeing to poor objectives may make planning to achieve them impossible. In well-designed competency frameworks competencies will be sufficiently independent to avoid this problem.
- No single simulation measures more than five competencies (ideally three).
- Simulations provide appropriate opportunity for competencies to be demonstrated equally by all candidates.

Commonly used simulations will not be, necessarily, the most effective, because not all commonly used simulations apply to all jobs. Because they are also limited in number there is a danger that selection processes include certain simulations only because they provide an opportunity to measure certain competencies, not because the activity simulated is found in the job.

Stand up and be counted

A call centre was recruiting staff to answer customer enquiries over the telephone. One of the essential competencies was identified as 'influencing others', and one of the exercises designed to assess this competency was a 10-minute presentation. Candidates were asked to prepare for this when they were invited to the selection interview.

Many candidates did not do well on this exercise because their presentation skills were not developed enough to allow their influencing skills to come to the fore. Because influencing through presentation was not part of the job, this exercise was hindering the selection process. In addition, the type of influencing that *was* required in the job was not being assessed.

Designing simulations for specific vacancies

A more focused, yet less restricted, way of identifying potential simulations is to match the competencies required in a job to key tasks that are to be performed in the job. In this way simulations can be developed that are unique to the vacancy.

Competencies provide one of the measures for identifying a simulation for a particular vacancy. For example, in our **Appendix Framework** (see page 134) the behaviours listed under 'Actively manages worthwhile relationships with customers' ('GROWS BUSINESS CAPABILITY: Customer Focus, Level 2') are:

- seeks feedback from customers to enhance services and/or products
- responds appropriately to customer requests
- establishes customer information needs in order to communicate effectively with customers.

These could be assessed using an exercise which simulates a meeting with a customer. The focus of the meeting and the level and type of customer involved would need to be identified using additional information about the vacancy – eg types of customers relevant to the role, current customer issues and examples of appropriate responses to customer requests.

Here is an example of how vacancy-specific simulations could be identified:

1 Identify the key tasks undertaken by job-holders – eg producing sales reports, co-ordinating project teams, conducting performance reviews, making presentations.
2 Identify the recruitment-critical competencies or competency levels.
3 Produce a grid of the competency levels and the key tasks.
4 Indicate which competencies/levels are critical, for which key tasks, by placing ticks in the grid.

An example of the type of grid that this process produces is shown in Table 8.

The grid is then refined in the same way as for generic simulations described earlier – that is, each competency should be measured at least twice, etc.

Table 8 *Grid showing the relationship between competency levels and key job tasks*

Key job tasks / Competency levels	Drafting project plans	Internal post	Team meeting	Project meeting	Project work	Meeting with clients	Staff mgmt meeting	Sales presentation
Builds relationships externally				✓		✓		✓
Supports team members			✓				✓	
Influences the thinking of others						✓		✓
Checks and analyses information		✓			✓	✓		✓
Ensures that decisions are made		✓		✓			✓	✓
Develops others			✓		✓			
Develops ideas into solutions	✓	✓		✓		✓	✓	✓
Plans to meet departmental objectives	✓				✓		✓	
Manages resources effectively	✓	✓		✓	✓			
Sets responsibilities			✓	✓		✓	✓	

Each column in the grid, for example in Table 8, can then be used to develop specific exercises. It may not be necessary to develop an exercise for each column – for example, it may be possible to measure all competencies at least twice using four or five exercises. Sometimes it is also possible to combine tasks in one exercise: internal post and report writing, for instance, could be combined in a business-reporting exercise.

To ensure that competency-specific evidence is collected using simulations, the simulations must be designed in a way that provides individuals with opportunities to demonstrate the competencies.

Prompts for examples of competencies can be built into:

- the instructions given to candidates and/or role players (ie briefings)
- the exercise activity (eg discussion or meeting)
- the outputs requested from the exercise (eg a report or presentation).

For example, assuming that competency levels have been identified for assessment and a simulated proposal presentation has been identified as one of the assessment exercises, the grid shown in Table 9 could be produced to ensure that relevant competencies are prompted by the design of the exercise. In this example the behavioural indicators from one competency level ('GROWS BUSINESS CAPABILITY: Improvement Focus: Level 3' from the **Appendix Framework** (see page 133)) has been entered. In practice, all behavioural indicators for all competency levels to be assessed using the proposal presentation would be entered into the grid.

Table 9 *Grid for incorporating competencies into a proposal presentation exercise*

Behavioural indicators	Briefing	Exercise activity	Outputs required
Responds positively to challenges from others			
Offers new ideas and solutions to current challenges			
Tests new ideas with others			
Readily adopts new ways of working			

Using the grid in Table 9, the designer of the assessment simulation exercise considers how examples of each behavioural indicator on the left might be prompted within the exercise. For example, the indicator 'Responds positively to challenges from others' could be prompted by ensuring that the presentation audience, eg one or more assessors, is briefed to challenge the candidate's proposals. The briefing to the candidate might prompt examples of 'offers new ideas and solutions to current challenges' by asking the candidate to propose solutions to issues stated or implied in the presentation brief. 'Tests new ideas with others' might be expected to be observed without prompting. 'Readily adopts new ways of working' might be prompted in the exercise brief – possibly by making the presentation proposal focus on the introduction of new ways of working.

The designer reviews each of the behavioural indicators and considers at which point in the exercise it will be most appropriate to prompt and/or observe examples of the behaviour. Notes on how the behaviour will be prompted are written into the relevant cells of the grid. When prompts for all behavioural indicators have been considered, the notes in the cells of the grid will provide a draft for the exercise.

A picture paints a thousand words

A public utility was designing a selection process for civil engineering supervisors. The job involved a number of key activities, including safety checks at building sites.

Simulations were designed around each of the key activities. For example, one simulation provided candidates with photographs of actual worksites. In this simulation the photographs contained a variety of good and poor working practices. Candidates were asked to report their observations and recommendations using brief notes – the same form of reporting that would be required in the job.

All the simulations were reviewed by existing supervisors and trade union representatives. The simulations were unanimously endorsed as representative of the vacancies, and full support was given to their use and the decisions made when using them.

The process is completed for each simulation until all competencies or competency levels can be assessed at least twice.

The key outputs that job-holders will be expected to produce in the job – eg levels of sales, new project developments or staff management – will help with exercise design. As indicated above, exercises can be designed to prompt candidates to produce outputs similar to those that would be required in the job.

For a particular assessment exercise, such as the example illustrated by Table 9, the design process described above can help to produce behavioural indicators specific to the particular job and to the behaviours expected to be observed in the exercise. For example, the generic indicators for 'GROWS BUSINESS CAPABILITY: Improvement Focus: Level 3' are:

- responds positively to challenges from others
- offers new ideas and solutions to current challenges
- tests new ideas with others
- readily adopts new ways of working.

Assessors may be asked to look for examples of the following:

- engages positively with challenges from the audience
- provides practical solutions to the implimentation issues raised in the presentation brief
- asks the audience for their views on the ideas presented in the presentation and/or proposes to survey staff on his or her proposals
- identifies ways to overcome resistance to the proposed new ways of working.

Providing role/exercise-specific behavioural indicators for each assessment exercise undertaken by applicants will ease the load placed on assessors.

Assessment centres for selection

An assessment centre, although often presented as an assessment tool or technique, is actually a process. The process uses a combination of some or all of the assessment exercises described above. What makes it different from other selection processes (which may also use a combination of the above exercises) is the way in which it is organised. In fact, it is better described as a multiple assessment process (MAP) in which there are:

- multiple participants
- multiple assessors
- multiple exercises
- multiple criteria.

To maximise objectivity, a MAP is organised so that every participant does every exercise and is seen/assessed at least once by every assessor.

The points made in this chapter regarding the contributions that competencies can make to selection processes also apply to assessment centres.

Using competencies as benchmarks for decision-making

Evaluating evidence of competency requires clear and unambiguous decision rules. It is essential that these rules are set up before decisions begin to be made in order to prevent unfair biases from creeping in later. Ad hoc changes to decision rules late in the process will reduce the consistency and accuracy of selection decisions. As with all other elements of selection, decision rules should be tested before they are used in order to ensure that they provide effective, appropriate and fair discrimination between candidates.

Assessment decisions should be both reliable and relevant to the vacancy. Assessment decision rules must be defined before selection commences and applied consistently after evidence of candidate competency has been collected. In competency-based selection these decisions usually apply to:

- turning evidence into competency ratings
- combining competency ratings from different exercises
- turning competency ratings into accept/reject decisions.

Turning evidence into competency ratings

Rating scales are normally used to assign scores to evidence of competency. In selection, the rating scale can be short, because evaluation usually focuses on evidence of acceptable or unacceptable competency. Typically, scales range from three rating-points to five rating-points; only one scale should be used throughout the process. Examples of scales are shown below:

Examples of rating scales		
A. Acceptable	1. Fully meets the standard	5. Outstanding
B. Marginal	2. Acceptable	4. Good
C. Unacceptable	3. Marginal	3. Acceptable
	4. Poor	2. Marginal
		1. Unacceptable

The more scale-points there are, the easier it will be to refine decisions about who should proceed to the next stage of selection. For example, the four-point scale allows for a decision rule such as 'Applicants who obtain a rating of one on all competencies will progress to the next stage, followed by applicants who achieve ratings of one and two with a majority of one ratings,' and so on.

Scale-point descriptions must be both meaningful and justified – eg 'acceptable' must be defined in terms of the evidence sought for the competency, such as 'Effective examples of most behaviours with no negative examples and no important omissions', and this should correspond with acceptable performance on the competency in the target job. Table 11 (see page 69) illustrates this point.

The primary task of the assessor is to match reported behaviour (eg from application forms or interviews) or observed behaviour (eg from tests or simulations) to examples of behaviour in the recruitment-critical competencies.

Competency ratings are produced in two ways:

- converting scores from tests and questionnaires
- comparing written evidence with behavioural indicators.

Competency-based questionnaires, such as those used for job applications, are relatively straightforward because a competency score can be linked directly to a competency rating. The rules for doing this are usually established when the questionnaire is trialled. For example, trialling might indicate that poor performers usually score between 0 and 3 on the questionnaire for a particular competency, while good performers usually score between 11 and 15 for that competency. Table 10 provides an example of rules compiled for converting scores to ratings. It is worth noting that different tables may be required for each competency because good performers may, for example, produce scores in a different range on each competency.

Table 10 *Example of converting test or questionnaire scores to competency ratings*

Questionnaire score	Competency rating
0–3	4. Poor
4–10	3. Marginal
11–15	2. Good
16–20	1. Outstanding

Scores obtained from psychometric tests and questionnaires can also be converted using the approach shown in Table 10. However, there are some complications, because psychometric tests and questionnaires do not usually provide direct measures of competencies and often contribute to more than one competency.

Diagnosing differences

A pharmaceutical company ran a series of internal assessment centres that used simulations and ability tests. It was noticed that candidates occasionally scored well on numerical reasoning tests but were not rated highly on competencies where analysing numerical information was important. This was creating a lot of discussion among assessors because they were having difficulty trying to assign an overall competency rating for 'analytical reasoning', based on low competency ratings from exercises and high scores from the test.

Because the assessment centre was internal it was possible to follow up the differences between test performance and competency ratings with individuals. It was established that individuals who performed well on the test, but not on the competency, required additional skills to put their numerical reasoning ability (as measured in the test) into practice with work-based tasks.

Following this finding it was decided to continue to use tests, but not to integrate them with ratings of competency. Test scores were used to identify potential that could be realised through targeted development.

If scores from psychometric tests and questionnaires are to be used to produce competency ratings, the relationship between test scores, specific competencies and competency ratings must be established. This is a task that requires specialist expertise.

Alternatively, and as preferred by the authors, scores from these measures can be left out of the overall competency assessment. Scores can then be used to interpret the overall assessment.

A lot of assessment evidence will be in the form of written information. Written information will be provided by the applicant – as in open-format application forms or written output from an exercise – or contained in the written notes produced by assessors when observing or interviewing the candidate.

Typically, assessors read through the written evidence from a particular assessment method. Pieces of evidence are then classified, using behavioural indicators as a guide, according to the competencies for

Table 11 *Example of converting written evidence to competency ratings*

Evidence	Rating
No opportunity given to demonstrate competency	**NE. No evidence**
Multiple effective examples of all behaviours with no negative examples	**1. Outstanding**
	2. Good
Effective examples of most behaviours with no negative examples and no important omissions	**3. Acceptable**
	4. Marginal
Multiple negative examples of behaviours with no positive examples and/or with important omissions	**5. Unacceptable**

which the exercise was designed. The quality and volume of the evidence per competency is then translated to a competency rating. Table 11 provides an example of rules compiled for converting written evidence to ratings.

Note that in Table 11 only the first, third and fifth rating-points have been defined. This makes the assigning of ratings much easier for assessors and reduces the incidence of split ratings: eg 2/3 and 3/4 or 3+ and 3−. The NE rating should be included in the scale but will not normally be used where exercises have been designed specifically to ensure opportunity is given for a candidate to demonstrate particular competencies. NE ratings are most likely to be given for group-based assessment exercises, eg group discussions and in interviews where the interviewer fails to ask or follow up on questions.

There is a significant difference between evaluating application evidence and evidence collected using other methods. Generic behaviours may be more appropriate for evaluating application evidence due to the limited information that can be collected. Evidence from other assessment methods can be evaluated using more detailed vacancy-specific and exercise-specific behaviours.

Combining competency ratings from different exercises
In the case of selection processes which use a combination of assessment methods/exercises, there will be more than one rating for each competency. There are two main ways in which several ratings for a competency can be combined to produce a single 'overall' rating for the competency. One method is to average the ratings obtained for the competency. Alternatively, assessors discuss the evidence for each rating of the competency and reach consensus on an overall competency rating.

The latter can be more meaningful because differences between ratings for a competency can be explored. For example, high and low ratings may have been given for a particular competency. On exploring the evidence behind each rating it may emerge that the higher ratings were too lenient. Assessors may therefore assign an overall competency rating lower than that which would be obtained by averaging.

The consensus approach also has the advantages that:

- Overall ratings are whole numbers, often using the same scale used for assigning ratings to competencies within exercises, eg Table 11.

- The development needs of individuals are often identified during these discussions.
- The discussions can be used to prepare for feedback.

It is essential that assessors are trained in how to combine ratings to produce a single overall rating for each competency.

It is only when a single rating has been produced for each competency that assessors move on to decision-making.

Turning ratings into decisions

Rules are applied to overall competency ratings to identify which applicants or candidates are to pass on to the next stage of selection. Selectors need these rules to ensure a consistent approach when interpreting sets of competency ratings. Rules may be different at different stages in the selection process, but, for consistency, it is important that they are established and agreed before the recruitment process is implemented.

As with the definitions of rating-points, decision rules should correspond to job performance, eg if it is essential that a job-holder demonstrates acceptable-to-outstanding performance in all the competencies, the decision rules must reflect this.

Different decision rules may apply where applicants are being screened following receipt of applications and where candidates are being accepted or rejected following more detailed assessments. Rules used at the application stage are likely to be more lenient than rules applied after extensive assessments, because information available at the application stage is limited.

Rules for shortlisting applicants should be set by comparing scores obtained on the competencies by existing job-holders with how well the job-holders are rated in terms of other job performance criteria. This approach requires large numbers of job-holders to establish that the decision rules actually relate to meaningful differences in levels of job performance. Test design skills and expertise with statistics are required to establish these rules. Where there aren't large numbers of job-holders, decision rules may need to be set by considering the impact of different degrees of competency on the potential to fulfil the job purpose. An accurate job profile and the views of job experts can be used to do this (see **Appendix 3** for a process for role profiling).

Table 12 shows a set of rules that could be used for open-format applications where, for example, four competencies are investigated and a four-point rating scale has been used (1 = poor, 2 = marginal, 3 = acceptable and 4 = outstanding).

In this example the rules would be applied in top-down order – ie 'fail' applicants are identified and removed from the applicant list. Next, the 'reserve' applicants are identified, followed by 'recommends'.

Table 12 *Example of rules used to sift application forms with four competencies*

Fail	Applicants rated '1' on any competency or more than two '2's
Reserve	One or two ratings of '2'
Recommend	Two or three ratings of '3'
Pass	Three or four ratings of '4'

This will leave the 'pass' applicants. If there is a quota for passing applicants to the next stage and the number of applicants who 'pass' falls short, then high-scoring 'recommends' might be added to the 'pass' list, followed by lower-scoring 'recommends'. If the quota is still short, the higher performers on the 'reserve' list could be added.

Table 13 is an example set of rules which might be used after detailed assessment of applicants (based on a five-point scale where 1 = outstanding and 5 = poor).

Table 13 *Example of rules for use after detailed assessment*

Accept candidates who obtain ... *Accept rules are applied in order, moving down the opposite column, until the target number of candidates have been accepted. If applying these rules does not produce a sufficient number of recruits, then top up using the 'hold' rules.*	all '1's; mostly '1's and '2's on others; mostly '1's and '2's with a few '3's; all '2's; mostly '2's and '3's with a few '1's; mostly '3's with a few '1's and '2's; all '3's.
Hold candidates who would be acceptable but for ... *If 'hold' candidates are required for the recruitment quota, individual candidates should be selected in order of the 'accept' rules (in the order above right) plus the one or two '4's rule – eg first select candidates with all '1's except for one or two '4's; next select candidates with mostly '1's and '2's with one or two '4's; and so on.*	one or two '4's.
Reject candidates who obtain ... *Rejected candidates must not be upgraded to 'accept'.*	more than two '4's and/or any '5's.

Providing feedback from competency-based assessments

The competency ratings and evidence of competency from different assessment methods can be used to provide assessment feedback to candidates after selection decisions have been made.

Feedback is most helpful for people when it can be used to help them understand selection decisions and/or put together a development plan for the future. Competencies enable feedback to be based on descriptions of behaviour, rather than simply a list of ratings. Feedback based on observations of performance against competencies also encourages a more accepting and positive atmosphere because evidence is being provided, rather than opinion.

One way of structuring feedback is to describe how a candidate performed in each competency overall and to illustrate with examples from the specific assessment exercises used in the selection process, eg 'Overall your leadership was rated acceptable – in the group discussion you were rated marginal, as you were unable to influence the direction of the discussion; however, you were rated highly in the team meeting where your colleagues readily acccepted your suggestions for overcoming the difficulties presented in the brief'. This type of feedback will be useful for successful candidates who wish to put together a development plan based on competencies.

Another way of structuring feedback is to describe how a candidate performed in each assessment exercise, breaking perfomance down by competency, eg 'You were very effective in the group discussion where you were able to use your business focus to balance the needs of the group with external commercial pressures – you also demonstrated effective leadership during this exercise when the group was unclear about its objectives and you took time to help them understand what was required.' This type of feedback is more useful for unsuccessful candidates who often find it easier to relate their performance to assessment exercises rather than to competencies.

All feedback should cover performance on all competencies assessed, and strong performance should be given equal weighting with development needs.

Monitoring competency-based selection

Competencies can play a useful role when monitoring the decisions and actions taken during selection. Records of selection decisions and ratings of competency, if regularly reviewed and acted upon, can help organisations to improve their selection processes by:

- preventing unfair selection decisions
- maintaining, or improving, the effectiveness of selection decisions.

Records of the ratings that individual applicants and candidates received against competencies can be used to assess:

- fairness – eg how assessors assign ratings to evidence
- how well individuals who received high scores on competencies subsequently performed, using these competencies, in the job.

In addition, retaining examples of competency provided by candidates on each assessment exercise will assist in reviewing the effectiveness of the assessment exercise. This information will help reviewers to check that the range of behaviour that the exercises were expected to generate has actually been observed and recorded.

KEY POINTS

- Selection assesses the match between people and job demands in order to place people into appropriate jobs.
- Effective selection requires use of appropriate criteria, appropriate assessment methods and decision rules.
- Competencies can contribute to selection by:
  - providing behavioural selection criteria
  - helping to phrase job advertisements
  - identifying and helping to design assessment exercises
  - providing benchmarks for selection decisions
  - helping to monitor selection processes.
- Selection can be based on recruitment-critical competencies.
- Desirable competencies can be used to choose between otherwise equally qualified candidates.
- Competencies are just one form of criteria that support the selection process.
- The overall effectiveness of a selection process does not depend solely on competencies. It

takes more than the introduction of competencies to a selection process to improve selection decisions.

■ The quality and relevance of assessment exercises, rating scales, decision rules, the selection process and the quality of assessors' skills are critical factors in the overall quality of selection decisions.

REFERENCES AND READING

PEARN KANDOLA (1996) *Tools for Assessment and Development Centres*. London, Institute of Personnel and Development.

Using competencies to review performance

In this chapter, reviewing performance is seen as a part of performance-management processes and refers to *all* situations in which the performance of an individual is reviewed, not just appraisal interviews. Reviewing performance might be a self-review or it could involve one or more others. This chapter does not include acting on outcomes from the review. Addressing underperformance and enhancing performance are dealt with in Chapter 6 (**Using Competencies for Training and Development**).

Performance reviews require skill to do well and they require tools to help manage the process – eg for collecting and structuring information. This chapter outlines how competencies can be used as a tool to help enhance both the design and the use of performance-management processes.

THE PURPOSE OF REVIEWING PERFORMANCE

There are many reasons for the performance of job-holders to be reviewed. From an organisational point of view these include:

- managing poor performance – identifying training and development needs for the current role
- identifying training and development needs for future roles
- motivating staff (eg setting challenging and stretching objectives, and providing positive feedback)
- rewarding performance (either through pay or some other reward)
- reinforcing stated organisational values and culture
- succession-planning (identifying individuals capable of moving to other jobs in the future)
- auditing (finding out what strengths and development needs exist in the organisation).

From an individual's point of view these include:

- identifying how well he or she is performing in his or her job
- identifying training and development needs for the current job
- rating performance for reward
- identifying potential to move on to another job.

In summary, performance reviews – while addressing many of the above needs – focus on one or more of the following purposes:

- establishing levels of performance
- identifying needs for performance improvement
- identifying development potential for succession
- discussing career interests/direction.

WHAT CONSTITUTES A PERFORMANCE REVIEW?

Performance reviews are often part of a larger process (eg appraisal and career planning). These larger processes frequently begin with setting objectives and action plans based on the requirements of the job and the abilities and development needs of the job-holder. The process then continues with interim reviews that monitor and revise action plans – in the form either of modified objectives or of a training and/or development plan. The process usually culminates in a formal review or appraisal of performance against both the objectives and the action plans.

Typically, performance reviews take place as one-to-one discussions between a job-holder and his or her manager or supervisor. However, reviews can also be conducted by teams or as a solo activity.

Increasing emphasis on teamwork has resulted in moves to review team performance as well as, or instead of, individual performance. Empowered teams may well be left to manage themselves in relation to who does what and how – a major measure of success being the achievement of team-set targets.

Whatever form the review takes, it will usually contain feedback on a job-holder's performance. It may be against pre-set objectives, behaviours and/or action plans. This may involve performance feedback from a range of people, from the job-holder to his or her manager, peers, direct reports and customers.

THE CONTRIBUTION OF COMPETENCIES TO REVIEWING PERFORMANCE

Competencies can make significant contributions to each of the purposes listed earlier, ie:

- establishing levels of performance
- identifying needs for performance improvement
- identifying development potential for succession
- discussing career interests/direction.

These contributions can clearly be seen in the steps which all performance reviews appear to have in common. No matter how complex or simple the review process, all forms of reviews usually follow a similar structure:

- identifying factors relevant to performance in the job
- collecting information on performance
- organising the information
- discussing or reviewing (eg for solo reviews) the information
- agreeing outcomes.

Identifying factors relevant to performance in the job

Once in the job, an individual will have specific targets or objectives that he or she must achieve (eg the number of units produced, items sold or calls answered). The more specific and measurable an objective or target, the easier it is to review that aspect of the performance of a job-holder. Targets and objectives may contain (we would argue that they *should* contain) specific and measurable outcomes. These outcomes are measurable indications of a job-holder's progress towards fulfilling the purpose of the job and are one type of job-performance measure.

A performance review might focus only on how well an individual has progressed towards meeting his or her targets or objectives. However, performance is no longer seen just as 'what' a job-holder achieves. Job performance is seen also to be about 'how' the job is carried out (eg the behaviour exhibited by the job-holder). Many organisations now review both what is achieved and how it is achieved when assessing job performance.

You get what you reward

A major international company expressed concern about poor relationships between one of its subsidiary companies and its partners abroad. A major objective of the subsidiary company was to guide the marketing of its parent company's key products in international markets.

Within the subsidiary company all customer-facing sales and marketing staff were set performance targets, based on sales volumes. Individuals were then appraised and rewarded according to performance against these targets. Sales met their target but customer complaints were rising and satisfaction of its international partners was plunging. Job-holder performance was reviewed only at annual appraisals in which the main focus was on assessing outputs and setting new output targets. Everything was aimed at short-term gains (outputs) without concern for how those gains were achieved, to such an extent that the future of the sales and marketing company was at risk.

In contrast, a public-sector organisation replaced its traditional appraisal process with a performance-review process based solely on competencies. This was founded on the belief that if a person does things in the 'right' way, they must produce the right outcomes. At first this might seem quite logical. However, competencies do not explicitly state what has to be done, nor do they define responsibilities or expected outcomes. Focusing performance reviews only on competencies (inputs) left individuals without clear direction, and disagreements arose about tasks and responsibilities.

These examples illustrate that problems can arise when performance reviews take too narrow a view of performance. Narrow views of performance inevitably lead to an underestimation of factors relating to or influencing job performance. This in turn undermines the potential benefits of reviewing performance as a whole.

Once an individual is in the job there is a lot of information available to help review their performance. For example, a job-holder could be reviewed against all aspects of his or her job, such as:

- producing things (eg products or decisions)
- fulfilling responsibilities (eg the management of others)
- behaving in a way that is acceptable within the organisation
- operating within particular contexts and environments
- dealing with other people
- operating pieces of equipment
- operating processes and procedures.

Although it might be possible to collect performance information on each of these areas, it is more usual to summarise performance into just two areas: the achievement of objectives or outputs, and behavioural performance – ie what the person achieves and how they achieve it. Behavioural performance information can be collected using direct evidence of competency, ratings of competency or feedback on competency observed by those close to the job.

Competencies provide a structure for collecting evidence of behavioural performance. At this stage in the process (identifying factors relevant to performance) it is necessary to identify the competencies and the levels of competency (if relevant) that are required in the job being reviewed.

Restricting the collection of competency performance information to competencies critical to performance at the required level reduces both time and effort in collecting the information. Therefore, rather than looking at the whole competency framework the review should just focus on the competencies needed for the specific job being reviewed, eg those listed in a competency-based job profile. This restriction also makes it easier to maintain a focus on important behavioural performance during the review discussion. A process for developing competency-based job profiles is provided in **Appendix 3**.

Competency-based job profiles should be developed through discussion with existing job-holders and their managers, because these individuals will have practical knowledge of the demands that the job places on job-holders. If a competency-based job profile already exists the job-holder and manager should at least discuss and check that it is still relevant, ie that changes have not occurred that alter the profile of competencies needed to deliver the job purpose.

Finally, it is important to be sure about the purpose of the performance review. For example, if a review is to assist in discussions about careers, the focus may be on competencies for future jobs/roles. However, reviews to establish levels of performance usually focus on competencies required in a current job/role.

Collecting information on performance

Once the competencies have been agreed, there are several ways in which information on behavioural performance can be collected.

The three basic forms of information that can be collected are:

- ratings of performance
- comments on performance
- examples of performance.

The type of information collected is likely to vary according to the availability of performance information and the purpose of the review. For example, many organisations use ratings of performance only where an overall performance rating is being sought as the outcome of the review – eg for pay reviews. However, other organisations collect comments only where the review purpose is to increase an individual's understanding of how he or she is perceived by others. Where an individual is new to a role, some organisations request individuals to undertake job-relevant assignments and to provide examples of outputs from the assignments.

Another way of collecting evidence of competency performance, widely used by many organisations, is to use an assessment centre process. This is justifiable for assessing competency performance for future or significantly changing roles or to select individuals for new roles. However, it is hard to justify using such a process to review performance relative to an individual's existing role – unless the normal performance-management and review process has not been used effectively, or where there are significant barriers to collecting on-the-job performance information. These assessment centres are often referred to as 'development centres', but this is an inaccurate description because the primary purpose is to assess performance and, by so doing, to assess individuals' development needs. We prefer to call this type of process an 'assessment-for-development centre' and cover this subject later in this chapter.

Assessment centres are discussed in Chapter 4 (**Using Competencies in Selection**) and development centres are discussed in Chapter 6 (**Using Competencies for Training and Development**). To retain the distinction between assessment centres for selection and those for identifying development needs, we refer to the latter as 'assessment-for-development centres' (ADCs) throughout this book.

Effective performance management and performance reviews should avoid the need to conduct assessments of an individual's current job performance using assessment centre processes. If a person is already doing the job, then information should be collected directly from the job using one, or a combination, of the following techniques:

- questionnaires
- records of achievement
- assignments.

To review performance relative to future roles or for career planning, the previous techniques may provide necessary information – but this could be supplemented with information from:

- assessment-for-development centres (looking at future roles)
- career review exercises.

Table 14 *Example of types of information and methods of collection used for different reviews*

Purpose of review	Forms of information	Methods of collection
To establish level of performance (current role)	Behavioural performance Output performance Task performance	Questionnaires Records of achievements Observations
To identify need for performance improvement	Behavioural performance Output performance Task performance Personal circumstances Organisational issues	Questionnaires Records of achievements Observations Discussions (eg with job-holder)
To identify development potential (future role)	Behavioural performance Output performance Task performance	Assessment-for-development centre Assignments
To discuss career interests	Work history Competency profile Aspirations Interests, knowledge and abilities Opportunities	Assessment for development centre Development centre Discussions with individual

In exceptional circumstances assessment-for-development centres may be required to collect evidence of performance for current job roles. Table 14 lists the different types of information and methods of collection that may be used for different reviews.

Collecting information using questionnaires

Questionnaires can be used to collect ratings of competency performance and they can also be used for collecting comments on competency performance. It is not always the case, however, that one questionnaire will collect both ratings and comments. Different questionnaires may be used to collect, for example:

- ratings against each behavioural indicator
- ratings against each behavioural indicator plus comments
- ratings against each competency
- comments on competency performance plus ratings against each competency
- comments on competency performance.

Because questionnaires are used to collect performance information about real job-holders in real jobs, the ideal questionnaires will be developed from the competencies necessary for effective performance in that job. Where an organisation has developed a competency framework, the framework should be used to develop the questionnaire.

'Off-the-shelf' competency questionnaires can offer a great deal of convenience where an organisation does not have a competency framework or where the framework does not cover the group of roles for which feedback is needed.

Features of off-the shelf questionnaires include:

- They are readily available.
- They are often machine-scoreable.
- Some provide comparisons with ratings obtained in other organisations.
- They provide professional looking reports.

But where a competency framework does exist, off-the-shelf questionnaires can pose problems. Matters that should be resolved when considering the use of such questionnaires include:

- Do they reflect the organisation's values/culture?
- Will they undermine confidence in the existing competency framework?
- Will users be distracted or confused by having more than one framework in use?
- What ownership will people feel for the content of the questionnaire?

The two main types of questionnaire used for collecting competency feedback, whether off-the-shelf or purpose-designed, are:

- ratings-based
- comments-based.

In the ratings-based type of questionnaire, raters are asked to rate each indicator of each competency. An overall rating is calculated for a competency by combining the ratings of the competency's indicators.

It is therefore important that the questionnaire enables raters to provide their best estimate of a job-holder's behavioural performance. This can be made easier by providing questionnaires that contain job-specific examples of the behavioural indicators – ie statements that describe how each behaviour would be observed in the particular job or role.

This type of questionnaire is often used where an overall rating of performance is being sought or a profile of the job-holder's competencies is being developed.

The indicators-based questionnaire can include sections for written comments, although they can make the questionnaire lengthy. If comments are particularly important, an alternative is to use a questionnaire in which the primary purpose is to collect written comments for each competency.

Another purpose of competency-based performance reviews is to provide the reviewee with insight into how he or she is seen by others. Although ratings-based questionnaires can be used for providing this feedback, it can be much more powerful when there are specific examples to illustrate why colleagues have given particular ratings.

Who said that?

Foreign exchange dealers in a major international bank attended a series of development workshops. During these workshops they were observed undertaking job-relevant tasks and they also received feedback on the tasks, as well as feedback from competency questionnaires completed by colleagues. Dealers frequently challenged observations of performance fed back by assessors. However, they readily accepted observations from their colleagues, taken from questionnaires, even though these simply confirmed the assessors' observations.

It can be useful to collect an overall rating for each competency with this questionnaire, because comments alone can be misleading.

The addition of a rating helps to ensure that comments are considered in the context of a view of overall competency. Without the rating there is a danger that positive or negative comments will be over-interpreted. Over-interpretation is especially likely where individuals in completing a questionnaire provide only one or two comments to highlight what they consider to be important issues.

When developing or choosing a questionnaire, careful consideration should be given to both the design of the questionnaire and its implementation. In particular, consideration should be given to:

- the length of the questionnaire
- its structure
- its rating scale
- who will complete the questionnaire
- managing the volume of questionnaires.

The length of the questionnaire – Experience tells us that most people do not like long questionnaires. It is therefore not a good idea to produce one questionnaire that includes all the behaviours in the competency framework. Many of the behaviours will not be relevant to specific job-holders being reviewed, and will waste time and distract raters.

Different jobs will have different competency profiles, so consideration must be given to producing job- or role-specific questionnaires. Where it is important that the review includes a detailed examination of competencies, and/or where detailed behavioural indicators already exist, a job-specific questionnaire may be justified. An alternative is to develop role-specific questionnaires – eg one for supervisory roles, one for administrative roles, and one for middle-managerial roles.

One way of producing job- or role-specific questionnaires is to organise the generic competency framework in a database or in word-processing files. The framework should be organised so that relevant job or role profiles can be printed out in a format appropriate for use in a questionnaire. For example, each competency level could be stored as a record in a database. It is then relatively easy to produce a job- or role-specific questionnaire by creating a file of behavioural indicators that correspond to the competency levels in the job or role profile.

Another effective approach is to administer the questionnaire on the computer screen. This can be done directly from a database. An advantage of this approach is that responses can be manipulated by the computer to produce feedback reports for the review discussion.

Automatic cover

A life assurance company introduced performance reviews for its sales staff. To facilitate the reviews a handbook was produced that included pencil-and-paper-based questionnaires and guidance for the review process.

After successful use of the handbook, the process was computerised. This enabled feedback questionnaires to be administered from the computer and for development profiles to be easily and automatically analysed.

The structure of the computer program enables updating of the competencies, and completely new competencies can easily be added. Because the computer contains the whole competency framework, new job-specific questionnaires are easily compiled.

Structure – Questionnaires are often designed in such a way that raters cannot easily tell which areas of performance specific questions relate to. However, in a competency framework some behavioural indicators (which will be converted into behavioural questions for the questionnaire) may be easier to interpret if it is evident which competency they relate to – eg, if behavioural questions are grouped under the relevant competency heading.

We have found that the most consistent ratings of competency for review are achieved when questionnaires are structured so that raters can clearly see which competency each indicator/question relates to.

Rating scale – Behavioural indicators are often rated using scales that require raters to indicate how effective they think the job-holder has been at using each of the behaviours, or how frequently the job-holder has used the behaviours effectively. Actual scales may vary depending on the specific application. For example, a major insurance company featured two scales in the same questionnaire – the first to indicate the frequency with which behaviours were used when needed, and the second to indicate how effective they were when used.

Because some raters may not have an opportunity to observe all the behaviours listed in the questionnaire, it is important that raters are able to respond 'cannot say' where appropriate. Each point of the rating scale must be clearly defined and definitions should be kept as simple as possible.

Tables 15 and 16 give two examples of rating scales.

In Table 16, raters are asked to use both scales to rate each behaviour. This approach enables more accurate ratings than Table 15.

Who will complete the questionnaire? – Questionnaires for performance reviews should be completed by individuals best placed to provide accurate feedback – ie those individuals with whom the job-holder's job requires regular interaction. When several people are asked to complete questionnaires relating to one reviewee, it is called a 'multi-rater' (sometimes alternatively called a 360-degree) process.

Table 15 *Example 1 of a rating scale for performance review*

Use the following scale to indicate how often and how effectively the person used each of the behaviours listed in the questionnaire:	
5 Cannot say	You have not been present in situations when the person needed to use the behaviour.
4 Very effective	The person used the behaviour effectively whenever a situation needed it.
3 Moderate effectiveness	The person used the behaviour in most situations which needed it and it was usually effective.
2 Marginal effectiveness	The behaviour was not very often used in situations that needed it, and/or when it was used it was not usually effective.
1 Poor effectiveness	The behaviour was not used in situations that needed it. Or if it was used, it was not effective.

Table 16 *Example 2 of a rating scale for performance review*

Use the following scales to indicate how often and how effectively the person used each of the behaviours listed in the questionnaire:			
Rating	**Frequency of use**	**Rating**	**Effectiveness**
5	No opportunity to observe		
4	All occasions when it was needed	4	Always effective
3	Most occasions when it was needed	3	Usually effective
2	Very few occasions when it was needed	2	Occasionally effective
1	Never, even though situations needed it	1	Never used effectively

Research indicates that multi-rater feedback can be affected by how confident the rater is that his or her feedback is going to remain anonymous. Perhaps it is not surprising that when raters believe they might be identified as the source of a low rating they tend to moderate their feedback scores. In general, this finding does not apply to the job-holder's manager, who in many feedback systems will be easy to identify. It has also been reported that job-holders tend to be more lenient when they rate themselves. However, we have found that this varies, depending on the purpose of the review. Where the review has a clear development purpose, job-holders often *underrate* their own performance.

Collecting feedback from several colleagues is more effective when it is reserved for special situations – for example, a development event or career review – or at least limited to the annual performance review. The job-holder can be left to choose whom he or she would like to complete questionnaires, and for development events this has proved very effective, because individuals often choose to apply for feedback from those who will not hide their opinions. A self-completion is almost always included, and other completions would include those of direct reports, peers, the manager and 'significant others'. Significant others have included customers and professional colleagues from outside the organisation. Including self-completion, seven to nine completed questionnaires are usually sufficient.

Questionnaires can also provide job-holders with a useful 'one-off' tool for self-review or for collecting the views of one or two individuals to review specific situations, such as individual roles within a project, or difficulties with particular working relationships.

Managing the volume of questionnaires – Competency questionnaires completed by several colleagues can produce a powerful review tool, but the tool can be weakened if the approach is used too often or if individuals do not have sufficient time to complete the questionnaires. In organisations where appraisals are scheduled within a narrow time-period, staff can get overloaded with requests for providing review feedback, because each individual may have several roles:

- job-holder
- peer to several colleagues
- manager
- internal supplier
- internal customer
- project team member.

Not only does this mean that an individual could be asked to complete 10 or more questionnaires, it also means there could be 10 times as many questionnaires in circulation than numbers of staff. If all appraisals are happening within an annual pay review period, these questionnaires will be distributed and will be circulating during a very short time-period. Add to this issues of confidentiality while keeping track of which questionnaires have been completed, and it becomes clear that a process is needed to manage the distribution and collection of questionnaires.

Computer-administered questionnaires can alleviate the administrative load, provided that confidentiality is built into the process. A tracking system of some description will be necessary to enable the chasing-up of tardy respondents.

It's in the post

A major FMCG company decided to introduce 360-degree feedback into the performance review process.

The numbers of staff made the task appear quite daunting. There were particular concerns about managing the volume of questionnaires and chasing up slow completions without undermining confidence in the confidentiality of the process. In addition, the organisation had a generic competency framework covering all jobs. However, the organisation did not want to have one competency questionnaire to cover all jobs: three hundred and sixty-degree feedback would be much more effective if questionnaires were based on the appropriate competencies and levels for each specific job. This meant, potentially, a unique questionnaire for every job role. The solution was to develop and install a competency-based 360-degree feedback system on the organisation's intranet.

The computerised solution was designed to enable unique, job-based competency questionnaires to be generated and completed online.

At the appropriate time in the review cycle, individuals received standardised e-mail requests for feedback. The e-mail provided information on who feedback was required for and a direct link to the appropriate place on the intranet for completing the questionnaire. Monitoring of completions could be done electronically without breaching confidentiality.

The system was launched as a trial with a small group of managers. However, news quickly spread and the system was rapidly adopted by the rest of the organisation.

Collecting information using records of achievement

Organisations are extending the use of the record of achievement – eg learning and development diaries – to include examples of behavioural performance for a wide range of staff. These examples may be actual outputs – eg copies of letters or reports – or they may be written summaries of how the individual has dealt with specific situations using the job competencies.

It is important, when using records of achievement, to train both the reviewer and the job-holder collecting the information. Reviewers and job-holders need to be aware of the type of information required and the quality. This will reduce the chances of collecting huge volumes of relatively useless paperwork.

This material lends itself to a wide range of performance reviews – for example, solo reviews of performance, discussion with peers or team, or review with manager and/or coach/mentor.

It's quality, not quantity, that counts

In one public-sector organisation, records of achievement were introduced. The training required the staff to be briefed about what sort of information would be needed. Three months later an assessor was presented with a file 80mm (slightly more than 3 inches) thick – full of paperwork to back up one competency.

The training was then amended to cover quality. As a visual demonstration two files were held up, one 80mm thick, and the other a much slimmer 16mm thick (less than three-quarters of an inch). The trainer announced that both files contained enough information to assess the same competency – and for everyone concerned the thinner file was the preferred one.

Collecting information using assignments

An assignment is a work-based project or task designed to allow an individual to demonstrate his or her competencies in relevant circumstances. Assignments can be useful for reviewing performance against current or future roles. They are used for current roles when an individual:

- has not been in a job long enough to obtain work examples
- is taking, or has taken, on new responsibilities
- has had mixed feedback about performance in a particular area of the job.

Because each competency can contribute to effective completion of more than one key job activity, assignments will usually enable collection of information on more than one competency.

Assignments must be carefully specified to ensure that tasks within them are representative of the job being reviewed and that these tasks provide adequate opportunities for observing and recording competency-relevant behaviours.

Individuals who undertake assignments can be given guidelines for the recording of behaviours, the approach and the outcomes during the assignment. Interpretation of the behaviours, approach and outcomes may be done solo, using written guidelines, or it could be reviewed in a team setting, or a one-to-one setting.

Collecting information using assessment-for-development centres (ADCs)

The purpose of an ADC is to identify what an individual would have to learn, or to improve on, to be considered a suitable candidate for another job or particular development scheme. In exceptional circumstances ADCs are used to assess development needs within the current job. Assessment centres for selection are covered in Chapter 4 (**Using Competencies in Selection**). Centres which are based on assessment centres, but which do not result in competency scores, and which are primarily for participants to practise and get feedback on competencies, are development centres, which are covered in Chapter 6 (**Using Competencies for Training and Development**).

ADCs are usually events during which individuals undertake a number of assessment activities. An individual's performance in each activity is compared against a set of benchmarks. This comparison results in a profile that is fed back to the individual. The outcome of the ADC process is usually a performance development action plan which addresses those areas in which the individual's performance fell short of the benchmark.

Competency frameworks can be used as:

- an aid in the design of the ADC activities
- the benchmark against which performance is measured
- the framework for discussing outcomes with the individual.

These points are expanded below.

There are two things that can be done to improve the contribution which competencies make to the design of ADCs:

1   Identify the competencies or competency levels which are essential for effective performance in the target job or group of jobs or critical for success on a development programme. Where the ADC is targeted at a future job the competencies will be those that make up the competency-based job profile. Where the ADC is targeted at a group of jobs the ADC competencies may just be the competencies common to all jobs in the group or they may be all the competencies required across all jobs in the group. Where the ADC is targeted at a specific development programme, the competencies should be those that are critical for success on that programme. As ADCs are normally future-focused, the competencies should be reviewed for relevance in the future, ie against anticipated changes.

2   Identify detailed examples of the generic behavioural indicators – ie what these generic behaviours will actually look like in the target job, group of jobs or the development programme, in the future. See the 'Adapting an existing framework to meet specific needs' section in Chapter 3 (**Developing a Competency Framework**).

ADC activities are essentially the same as assessment activities for selection – that is, they allow observers to assess the levels of performance in an activity against agreed benchmarks. The principles of the design of such activities are also similar to those outlined in the 'Designing simulations for specific vacancies' subsection in Chapter 4 (**Using Competencies in Selection**) and we do not repeat them here. However, there are some important differences between the events that surround ADCs and those that surround assessment centres for selection. These are:

- benchmarking
- the scale of the event
- feedback.

In much the same way that they can be adapted for use in selection events, behavioural statements are used in ADCs. However, it is likely that a wider range of competencies and therefore more behavioural statements will be used – especially in cases where people are attending an ADC to assess potential for another job or level in the organisation.

An increased number of competencies and behavioural statements means an increase in the number of assessment exercises or activities that make up an ADC. ADCs are typically longer in duration than assessment centres for selection.

Another key difference between assessment centres for selection and ADCs is the emphasis on feedback during and after the event. In many ADCs the feedback is extensive and focuses on what was and was not observed rather than on ratings of performance.

ADCs place at least as much emphasis on understanding and diagnosing performance as they do on assessing it.

Organising the information

For indicator-based questionnaires, the overall score for each competency is calculated for each questionnaire (rater) before ratings from all questionnaires are combined to produce the feedback information. 'Cannot say' ratings should not be incorporated into the overall competency rating. 'Cannot say' ratings should be reported separately in the feedback because these can be useful pieces of information – especially if they are ratings given by raters who *should* be able to say!

When competency scores are collected from a group of colleagues (such as peers and direct reports), it is a relatively easy task to combine and analyse scores on each competency. This information can then be fed back graphically, as in bar charts, and it is easy to feed back comparisons of scores – eg how colleagues rated a reviewee on a competency and how his or her direct reports rated him or her on the competency. Figure 3 is an example of how scores can be illustrated using a bar chart.

Such a diagram is a useful presentation of competency ratings because it enables easy comparison between groups of raters, making it easy to identify significant differences between them. This is important because significant differences can occur when groups rate a competency, and these differences may be both valid and meaningful. For example, direct reports may have the best opportunities and experiences to provide the most accurate ratings of their manager's 'GROWS INDIVIDUAL CAPABILITY' competencies. A job-holder's manager may be in the best position to rate the job-holder on the 'Business Focus' competency and 'Customer Focus' competency.

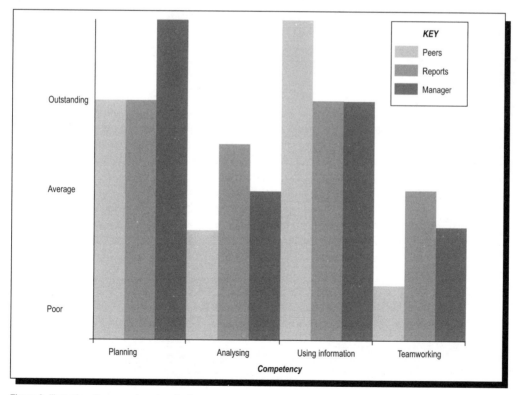

Figure 3 *Illustration of scores using a bar chart*

A separate overall rating can also be presented for each competency. Presenting this separately and in addition to ratings from the different rater groups reduces the potential to discard meaningful differences. Such differences can be lost if overall competency ratings only are produced. For example, a job-holder may have received an overall average rating for 'teamworking'. On surveying the ratings from different rating groups it may appear that peers and more senior colleagues have rated the individual at a little above average whereas members of the team that the individual manages have given consistently low ratings. This difference could be critical, indicating that the individual's approach to working with his or her team's members is below an acceptable standard.

Some competency-based feedback systems go much further and present a breakdown of ratings. This breakdown usually gives some indication of the spread of ratings obtained within each competency and within each rater group. Table 17 shows how this may be presented.

In this example there are nine raters, as indicated in the top row. For each competency the highest and lowest ratings are shown for each group of raters. This level of detail is useful when there is a dispute over the overall rating given to a competency. For example, it may be that direct reports tend to see a different side of their manager's 'leadership style' than do the manager's colleagues. This detail is also useful when diagnosing performance and when considering development.

A similar format can be used to summarise ratings by rater groups at the behavioural indicator level. At this more detailed level, the range of ratings can be displayed, as in Table 17, and the number of 'cannot say' ratings can also be included. Having both overall competency ratings and detailed indicator ratings makes it easier to prepare for the review discussion – eg key development areas within a competency can be discussed without losing sight of the fact that overall performance on the competency was rated acceptable.

Where examples of performance have been collected – eg records of achievement and assignments – they are usually evaluated/rated against the competencies before they are discussed. Rating guidelines are required to do this consistently.

Examples of competency from ADCs will usually be evaluated at the centre by the facilitators. Assignments and records of achievement may also be evaluated prior to the review discussion. These could be evaluated by the job-holder, if trained to do so, or by some other trained person. It is important not to reduce this information to a number (rating) which, compared with the examples, is relatively meaningless. It is the examples that are important, because they indicate the elements of a competency that may require training or development. If a person has been rated '3' overall for 'Planning', it may indicate that the person has a development need in this competency. Another person may be rated the same, but have a different development need in that competency. What is important for the review discussion is *why* the person was rated as having a development need. A good reviewer will have prepared evidence from the available examples to support his or her assessments of competency.

Table 17 *Example of spread of ratings per competency*

Raters / Competency	4 × Reports		3 × Colleagues		1 × Manager		Self	
	min	*max*	*min*	*max*	*min*	*max*	*min*	*max*
Managing relationships	3	4	2	5	3	3	4	4
Teamworking	4	4	3	3	3	3	4	4
etc								

When preparing feedback from questionnaires, the reviewer needs to prepare examples to illustrate ratings. In the comments-type questionnaire, examples can be selected from the comments to illustrate consistent themes: *both* strengths *and* development needs. Examples can even be prepared from the rating questionnaire. In this case preparation may focus on ratings of the behavioural indicators. Where a competency received an overall poor rating, it is important that the reviewer can quickly show which behaviours contributed to the poor rating – ie which behaviours were rated lowest – and, if appropriate, which rater groups rated them low.

Reviews should be balanced. Preparation should ensure that individuals are aware of actual and potential strengths as well as development needs. Preparation must not just seek examples to reinforce feedback of weaknesses or development needs.

One step forward, two steps back

A grant organisation ran a series of ADCs to assess the potential of staff for supervisory positions. The feedback from the ADCs was focused entirely on development needs. Unfortunately, this meant that participants felt deflated, hearing only messages about what they were not yet able to do – ie were not good at. The result was that instead of leaving the ADC looking forward to developing into a role, most participants left feeling that they would never make it.

Discussing the information

Performance review discussions require skill and good preparation. The reviewer should be someone who has a good understanding of both the purpose of the review and the review information, which will often contain information in addition to that on competency – eg performance on job objectives, service standards and career aspirations/opportunities.

Where a review follows an assessment centre for selection or an ADC, it is usually better if the review discussion is undertaken by a centre facilitator, because he or she will be intimately acquainted with the examples of performance. Ideally, ADC facilitators should be a mix of line managers and HR specialists. If reviews are based on feedback prepared on behalf of the reviewer, the reviewer must spend sufficient time getting to understand the information before the review discussion.

Although rating-type information is easier to present, this does not mean that it is easier to discuss. Rating information, usually in the form of multi-rater feedback, is becoming very popular. This may be because:

- it is easy to work with the data
- analysis of data is not as time-consuming as analysis of written information
- it is easy to present the information graphically
- agencies make this easy to produce.

Drawbacks to this form of feedback are that:

- it may appear more factual than is warranted
- raters will not have had equal opportunities to observe all behaviours
- behaviours may not be equally amenable to rating
- the reviewee focuses more on the scores than on the examples.

These points must be borne in mind and accounted for during the discussion. It may be that during the discussion examples are explored which result in changes to evaluations arrived at when preparing for the discussion.

As stated earlier, job performance is not just about outputs; nor is it just about behaviours or competencies. A thorough and meaningful performance review should also look at factors that affect an individual's ability to demonstrate appropriate behaviours and factors that influence the individual's ability to deliver the required job outputs. These factors relate to characteristics of the person, their personal circumstances and circumstances within the organisation. The relevance of specific personal and organisational factors to performance rarely becomes apparent until behavioural and output performance has been established. It is therefore usually during the discussion of performance information that these factors are identified and explored.

There are many factors which influence how job-holders behave and perform. Table 18 lists a number of them.

There are a few important points that reviewers need to keep in mind when feeding back a summary of competency ratings:

- It is easy for this form of review information to appear, or to be presented, as a series of facts – eg 'You are good at this' ... 'You are not so good at this.' This can be avoided by describing what was reported – eg 'You were rated highly on this area by ...'.
- The feedback summary is a very structured and condensed set of perceptions. It is not a definitive statement about the reviewee.

Table 18 *Examples of factors that can influence performance at work*

Factor	Examples
Domestic	❏ home life – ie family role, relationship issues ❏ other commitments – eg hobbies, studies, voluntary work
Organisational	❏ resources for work ❏ politics at work ❏ context – eg changes, uncertainty ❏ relationships ❏ culture ❏ role/task clarity
Managerial	❏ relationship ❏ support for the job ❏ support for the person ❏ changes
Personal	❏ abilities – mental and physical ❏ preferences ❏ values ❏ traits ❏ experience ❏ knowledge ❏ attitudes

- It is quite possible that some behaviours have been misinterpreted by raters, so it is important to identify them and to try to understand why they may have been misinterpreted.

- This form of review information is for discussion. It is a tool to check out the reviewee's view of his or her typical competency. The task is to find out how and why the review information fits or contrasts with the individual's own views.

- The examination of examples provided in discussion by the reviewee may result in a new view of the reviewee's competencies.

- Disagreements between groups of raters can be meaningful. It can be useful to explore disagreements during the review to develop an understanding about how they may have arisen – eg managers' views versus team members' views.

- Behaviours may not be equally amenable to rating. Some behaviours, such as those related to analysing information and decision-making, may not be easy for some colleagues – who may see only superficial aspects of some behaviours – to rate.

  One example of this in our **Appendix Framework** (see page 133) is the behaviour 'Uses knowledge of the external environment to maximise opportunities for the business' ('GROWS BUSINESS CAPABILITY: Business Focus, Level 1'). Many observers may have knowledge of the actions a reviewee has taken to maximise opportunities for the business, but few (if any) may have been close enough to know what information was used and what information was available.

These points reinforce the need to use competency-rating feedback as a basis for a discussion about the behavioural side of performance rather than as an assessment tool.

Solo/self-review

Not all performance reviews are conducted with another person or other people. It is possible for individuals to review performance information alone. If individuals are going to undertake solo/self-review, there should be very clear guidelines and training, where appropriate, to assist them through this process. The important points that reviewers need to keep in mind when feeding back information about competency ratings outlined above are particularly relevant here. If there is no one with whom an individual can discuss the outcomes, it may be easy for review information to be seen as 'the final word', rather than as a basis for exploring behaviour.

On the whole, performance review is better conducted with at least one other person, if only so that an alternative viewpoint or challenges can be put forward. Solo or self-reviews can, however, be beneficial in their own right, as well as helping individuals to prepare for discussion with others.

Agreeing outcomes

If an overall rating of the behavioural performance of an individual is required, it should result from a discussion of the questionnaire and other feedback – it should not come directly from questionnaires.

Annual performance reviews and appraisals usually feature an overall performance rating. Including competencies in the review process automatically raises the perceived importance of behaviour in job performance. As illustrated in the earlier example (page 76) **You get what you reward**, ignoring competencies when producing an overall performance rating reduces the perceived importance of behaviour.

A thorough assessment of performance therefore includes evaluations of both competency performance and achievement of outputs etc, taking account of both personal and organisational influences. Such an assessment often results in ratings for achievement of each output as well as ratings for each competency, especially when the review contributes to pay awards. This approach is often taken further to produce an overall rating for achievement of outputs and an overall rating of competency performance.

A third stage is sometimes included, which combines the overall rating of achievement of outputs with the overall rating of competency performance to produce one overall performance rating.

This approach results in three layers of ratings:

- individual ratings for competencies and for outputs
- overall ratings for competencies and for outputs
- overall performance rating.

For example:

- An individual has been rated on six targets and eight competencies
- Rating scales similar to those in Table 19 (opposite) are then used to establish an overall rating for outputs and an overall rating for competencies
- The two overall ratings are then combined to produce one overall performance rating.

Combining performance ratings

Organisations combine overall output and competency ratings to produce one overall performance rating in different ways. Three examples are:

1 Average the two ratings.
2 Produce an average after weighting one of the ratings: eg some organisations give more weight to outputs than to competencies.
3 Use a set of rules to limit the combined rating – eg to avoid a very low rating and a very high rating being averaged to produce a mid-level combined rating.

In the first example (average of ratings), an overall output rating of '5' and an overall competency rating of '3' would produce a combined rating of '4'.

In the second example, an overall output rating might be weighted by a factor of 2. So an overall output rating of '5' and an overall competency rating of '3' would produce a combined rating of '6.5' (5×2 [the weight] $= 10$, $10 + 3$ [the competency rating] $= 13$, $13/2 = 6.5$).

These approaches can produce odd combined scores. For example, the first approach would produce a combined rating of '3' for overall ratings of '1' and '5', the mid-point of a five-point scale. The definition of a combined rating of '3' may be 'acceptable'. However, the organisation may consider that anyone obtaining a rating of '1' cannot be considered acceptable.

The effect is less exaggerated with the second approach. For example, a rating of '1' on outputs and a rating of '5' for competencies would produce a combined rating of '3.5'. As the scale for combined ratings using this approach is 7.5 to 1.5, 3.5 is below the mid-point.

In the third example a set of rules is applied to recognise the presence of low ratings. Table 20 illustrates how ratings could be combined.

This approach produces a combined rating of 2 for overall ratings of '1' and '5', acknowledging that overall performance is considered poor.

Table 19 *Example of rating scales*

	Outputs	Competencies
5	Exceeded standards required on all targets	All competencies rated 'outstanding'
4	All targets achieved to required standards: some exceeded	A mix of 'good' and 'outstanding' ratings
3	Most targets achieved to required standard	Most competencies rated 'good'
2	Many targets achieved close to standard; a few not met, but progress made	Most competencies rated 'marginal'
1	Very few or no targets achieved to standard	Most competencies rated 'poor'

Table 20 *Combining overall ratings*

Overall ratings	Combined rating
5 + 5	5 – outstanding
5 + 3, 5 + 4, 4 + 4	4 – good
5 + 2, 4 + 3, 3 + 3	3 – acceptable
5 + 1, 4 + 2, 4 + 1, 3 + 2, 2 + 2	2 – poor
3 + 1, 2 + 1, 1 + 1	1 – unacceptable

KEY POINTS

- Performance reviews may be undertaken for a wide variety of purposes.
- To be effective, reviews must focus on what an individual does (outputs), how he or she does it (behaviour), and the factors that may influence these things (personal and organisational factors).
- Reviews that focus on limited information do not produce a fair view of overall performance.
- Where used for reward, limited reviews are likely to encourage individuals to adopt a narrow view of what is important in their work.
- Competencies provide a useful focus for obtaining information on how a person goes about their work.
- Competency information can be collected in many ways and from a variety of people. This requires specialist tools and effective procedures to manage the volumes of both information and work that can be generated.
- Care must be taken when using competency information because questionnaire data, in particular, can be easy both to misinterpret and to misrepresent.
- To be meaningful, the data must be discussed in the light of what the person is trying to achieve as well as personal and organisational influences. It is also necessary to understand how and why others might have different perceptions of an individual's behaviour.

- Competencies provide a useful structure for feeding back or discussing behavioural performance.

- It is important when preparing information for a review discussion that the information is not reduced to numbers.

- Where ratings of behavioural performance are discussed, it is important that the purpose of the review is not forgotten. In many cases the purpose will be to ascertain and/or agree the level of an individual's performance, including areas for improvement.

- The purpose of most reviews is not to discuss behavioural performance, but to use the discussion to arrive at an overall view of performance, which then leads to some form of action – eg a development plan or a pay adjustment.

- A good review requires a good reviewer – someone who can effectively prepare performance information for discussion, evaluate the information against benchmarks and measurable targets, apply rating rules, explore (with the reviewee) any personal and/or organisational factors that may be affecting performance, integrate output and behavioural information with personal and organisational factors, and arrive at an agreed and fair assessment of overall performance.

- Competencies make an important contribution to performance reviews because they help structure and standardise discussions about how a person goes about doing their job. However, it is the successful combination of all the factors mentioned in this chapter (eg reviewers, review processes and use of other appropriate performance criteria) that make reviews good. A good competency framework will not, by itself, either make poor reviewers good or a poor review process good.

Using competencies for training and development

In this chapter we treat training as an aspect of development. We use 'training' to encompass activities and events that concentrate on the learning and practice of specific knowledge and techniques. We consider 'development' to be much broader and something that takes learning on to the development of skill and expertise.

This can be illustrated as follows:

'TRAINING' AND 'DEVELOPMENT'

Joe decides that he needs to learn to drive. He takes a series of formal lessons with a driving instructor. He also goes out with his mother (who is an experienced driver) to practise in between his lessons. Joe passes his driving test at the first attempt.

Taking driving lessons and practising is Joe's 'training' – he learns and practises specific techniques. The fact that Joe has passed his test does not mean he is a skilful driver. It does mean that he was able to demonstrate that he understood, and could put into practice, the knowledge and techniques required to drive a car safely.

Over the following years Joe 'develops' his driving skills and expertise. He does this by applying the techniques he has been trained in to a wide range of different conditions and circumstances. Because he has learned from his experiences, he becomes a skilful driver.

THE PURPOSES OF TRAINING AND DEVELOPMENT

There are many reasons for training and development to be seen as important from both the organisation and individual perspectives. These reasons include the need for:

- people to stay employable throughout a lifetime during which jobs and careers may change – *a willingness to continue learning and developing is becoming an essential part of continuous employability*

- employees to learn methods and techniques required to do specific tasks – *eg people who are new to a job, people having to use new equipment, processes and procedures*

- the development of future successors – *minimising the costs of recruiting externally and maximising the benefits of keeping knowledge and experience in the business*

- increasing resources from existing staff – *increasing the capacity of people in the organisation to be skilled in more than one area*

- motivating, attracting and retaining key staff – *as fragmenting of the workforce (eg with the use of outsourcing and contract staff) continues, and as fewer people join the job market each year.*

Training and development therefore usually serve one or both of the following purposes in the pursuit of a successful organisation or career:

- to ensure that knowledge, techniques and skills meet current needs
- to ensure that knowledge, techniques and skills are prepared to meet future needs.

FACTORS THAT INFLUENCE TRAINING AND DEVELOPMENT

Training and development provided by an organisation

Factors that influence the training and development offered within an organisation include:

- organisational strategic plans – in particular any changes from current levels or types of business
- organisational policies – which may include the provision of events to identify needs (eg assessment-for-development centres) and/or a policy of encouraging learning *per se*
- career opportunities available within the function (eg support for progression within a profession through nationally recognised qualifications) or within the organisation (eg support for progression within the internal hierarchy through generic training such as in management techniques)
- future needs – the need to develop staff towards other roles (succession) or the need to develop staff to meet changes in the business (eg the introduction of new technology or an attempt to change culture)
- skills shortage – ie the skills of the current staff do not meet current requirements
- the need, or desire, to meet external requirements – to gain recognition of a commitment to training (eg Investors In People), to comply with legal and/or professional regulations (eg the Financial Services Authority or Control of Substances Hazardous to Health) or to secure funding (eg via government initiatives).

The aims of training cause many companies to take positive action to ensure that their staff are given opportunities to train and develop. As we can see above, however, there are many factors that influence what those opportunities are.

Training and development realised by an individual

The factors that influence how much learning *actually* takes place are environmental and individual.

Environmental influences include:

- availability of resources, both in terms of the number of people who can be 'released' at any one time to attend an event and in terms of the amount of budget available to pay for the events
- quality of the event – how formal or informal, structured or unstructured, events contribute to the objectives of the learner
- quality of post-event support – the level of support in helping the learner transfer learning to the workplace
- learning culture – how much an organisation promotes learning by seeing mistakes as opportunities to encourage people to improve their skills by learning from them.

Individual influences include:

- learning styles, preferences for different types of learning activity and previous experience of what works best for the individual
- motivation, based on the positive and negative reinforcements of what is accepted behaviour in the organisation

- personal needs – eg the ambition to learn to improve one's employment prospects, either within the organisation or outside it

- personal interests, based on what the person enjoys doing or wants to do to challenge himself or herself

- personal situation (ie what else is on the individual's mind) – personal circumstances may affect how well an individual can concentrate

- potential/current knowledge – eg does the person have the underpinning knowledge required as a prerequisite for the learning?

- abilities – is the person able, intellectually, to grasp the theories, concepts and so on that are being trained? And, for example, does the person have the necessary dexterity needed to be trained in certain physical tasks?

These lists, although not definitive, show that however much training and development is offered and is taken up, the actual learning that takes place is influenced by many different factors.

THE CONTRIBUTION OF COMPETENCIES TO TRAINING AND DEVELOPMENT

It used to be that training needs were met through identifying which relevant course someone could attend. The techniques that were learned may have been useful, but often did not address the underlying issues creating the need.

Competency is the result of the skilful application of several techniques in combination with particular attitudes, values, abilities and knowledge. For example, successful team-leading can be the result of effective training in such techniques as appraisal interviewing, management of meetings, feedback or performance management. But it also relies on, among other things, an interest in developing people, respect for individuals' needs, knowledge of the team members, and personal motivation to do a good job.

A well-designed competency framework adds the behavioural dimension to all elements of training and development. It will assist in:

- identifying needs
- structuring plans and programmes
- designing events
- selecting events and activities
- evaluating success.

Identifying training and development needs

There are several ways in which training and development needs can be recognised. These include:

- performance reviews – formal and informal
- multi-rater/360-degree reviews
- assessment exercises for selection
- assessment exercises for development
- self-review
- skills audit
- career-development interviews.

Whatever system is used, the basic principle remains the same: identification of training and development needs is about reviewing an individual's or organisation's performance against a benchmark. Where the benchmark is produced by a professional body, training and development needs will be identified across the members of that profession. Competencies help to define the behavioural elements of a benchmark by providing examples of what effective behaviours look like.

Most of the above methods of identifying training and development needs have been covered in either Chapter 4 (**Using Competencies in Selection**) or Chapter 5 (**Using Competencies to Review Performance**). These chapters cover how the outputs from performance reviews, assessment centres, etc can highlight an individual's training and development needs. Collation of the outputs from these activities can also highlight team-based or organisation-wide needs.

Chapters 4 and 5 do not cover skills audits and career-development interviews, which are covered here. These activities are as much to do with finding appropriate benchmarks as they are to do with comparing performance against them.

Skills audits

Skills audits are snapshots of the current competency levels in a particular business unit (from a team to the whole organisation). They are usually conducted with the primary objective of identifying training and development needs by comparing current competencies with those required now or in the future.

Depending on the number of people involved in the audit, the methods of collection might include:

- a review of training records
- questionnaires
- workshops
- interviews.

It is important for the purpose of the audit to be established, before it is carried out, in order to ensure that the correct amount of information is collected. For example, if a snapshot is required to get a feel for major areas of weakness in a company, a skills audit in which every member of staff is interviewed would probably be unnecessary, unless the organisation was very small. Questionnaires, workshops and interviews with key individuals (eg samples of managers and job-holders) may be more appropriate.

A review of training records may be carried out on the basis that the more popular the event, the more likely it is to be a common need. There is some truth in this, but information should be treated cautiously for two reasons. Firstly, it may be that the event is too generic to enable training needs to be accurately assessed. For example, a planning techniques course may be attended by people with poor planning skills as well as by people with poor time-management skills. Good evaluation data will go a long way towards addressing this issue. Secondly, training records only show what events people have attended. They do not show needs that are not being addressed or what training is actually being used back in the workplace. So, training records provide useful information but are always best supplemented with other information if they are to be used in a skills audit.

Competency frameworks can be used to structure skills audit questionnaires. Behaviours listed in each of the competencies can be used as statements against which people rate their own behaviour, or the behaviour of others if required. Table 21 shows how such a questionnaire may look using the behaviours for the **Appendix Framework** (see page 133) 'GROWS BUSINESS CAPABILITY: Improvement Focus' competency.

Table 21 *Example of skills audit questionnaire*

Listed below are a number of behaviours related to Growing Business Capability. Review each behaviour, and rate how frequently you feel your normal behaviour matches the description, using the rating scale shown.					
1 – always 2 – often 3 – sometimes 4 – rarely 5 – never	1	2	3	4	5
Seeks and promotes innovation to take the business forward					
Works to establish an environment where individuals feel opinions and ideas are welcomed					
Quickly translates ideas with potential business benefits into actions					
Champions change when it is required					
Encourages the sharing of experiences to improve performance					
Responds positively to challenges from others					
Offers new ideas and solutions to current challenges					
Tests new ideas with others					
Readily adopts new ways of working					

Questionnaires can be issued to:

- job-holders to complete – considering their own skills or the skills of their colleagues in general
- line managers to complete – considering the skills of their teams.

As questionnaires will be focusing on perceived 'weaknesses' it is important to establish anonymity. This is vital even when asking managers to rate their staff. It is not inconceivable for managers to rate their team leniently, particularly if they feel the team lacks key skills and yet he or she is the person responsible for their training and development. The purpose for completing the questionnaire should be made clear and supported throughout the process. Promises of 'no blame' should not be broken by making people feel that the finger is being pointed at them for the results of the audit.

Results from questionnaires can be explored further in interviews and/or workshops. Both methods can give useful insight into the reasons behind high or low scores on the audit. The purpose of an interview or workshop is to explore the reasons behind questionnaire results; the real experiences of interviewees or workshop attendees can be used therefore to ensure that results are not based on speculation.

Career-development interviews
A career-development interview is a structured discussion between an individual and another person about the individual's aspirations and prospects. We use the term 'career' to mean the progression of an individual from job to job in a way that will maximise current competencies and open up opportunities to develop competencies that will be useful in the future. Nowadays, a career may involve several sideways moves and changes in organisation, profession or sector.

An inexperienced counsellor might be tempted to focus on the professional or technical experience of a person and limit the search to jobs using that professional or technical knowledge. Focusing on specific expertise alone could limit someone's career choices unnecessarily.

Competencies add an important dimension to the career-development interview because considering known areas of strength in competencies can lead to a wider range of job opportunities. For example, the list of opportunities for someone with strengths in leadership may broaden to encompass jobs that are not necessarily in their familiar field of expertise, but which draw on those leadership skills.

People conducting thorough career-development interviews or discussions need information about the individual's competency profile. This can be obtained by any of the means mentioned at the beginning of this section (eg performance reviews, assessment exercises, etc). It is important, however, that any information gained through these methods is viewed with certain factors in mind:

- How objective is the information? Is it a self-report or others' observations of the individual's behaviour?
- How broad-ranging is the information? Selection assessments are likely to have been restricted to recruitment-critical competencies, and exercises for assessing development needs may have focused on the *current* job competencies. Both sets of assessment information will have left out competencies or competency levels relevant to *potential* jobs that differ from the current job.
- For what purpose was the information gathered? For example, selection events will concentrate on performance against prescribed benchmarks, and feedback may therefore not contain detail about which level of competency was reached.

Whatever the events that preceded the career-development interview, one outcome of the interview is likely to be the identification of an individual's training and development needs, and suggestions about how to meet those needs.

As well as identifying the need, competency frameworks also help identify whether the need is a training one or a development one. Assuming that a person needs to do a particular activity better and is willing to undertake the activity, two questions need to be answered, 'Do they know what to do?' and 'Do they know how to do it?' If the answer to either question is 'No', it is likely to be a (knowledge and/or technique) training need. If the answer to both questions is 'Yes', it is likely to be a (skills) development need. Competencies can also help identify what elements of behaviour need to be developed.

To illustrate how competencies can help identify different types of training and development needs, let us assume that someone was identified as needing to improve on 'SHOWS THE WAY: Planning Level 3' in the **Appendix Framework** (see page 133), ('Uses appropriate planning to succeed in own role'). It could be that the person simply does not know how to plan, and therefore a course in planning techniques may well be the answer. However, it could be that they know how to plan but they never consider the 'what ifs'. Development in this specific behaviour can then be targeted. Alternatively, the person may know how to plan but finds it hard to put all the behaviours together in the workplace. In this case, development in the whole competency can be targeted.

Structuring training and development plans and programmes

The intention to meet training and development needs is expressed in a learning objective. Learning objectives are essentially the same as any other performance objective – what is it that the individual, organisation or profession wants or needs to achieve, and how is it going to be achieved?

The 'how' of learning objectives translates into a plan of action. To meet organisation- or profession-wide needs, the plan will focus on combining events and activities within a programme to help people develop the skills required to raise the performance of the organisation or profession. At an individual level, an action plan will focus on events and activities to help the person develop the skills required to do their job or develop the skills demanded by an organisational or professional programme.

In this section we discuss a *structured* approach to meeting training and development needs at all levels. Organisations that identify needs and then hope that they will be met by sending people on a few courses are likely to be disappointed in the results. A structured approach to meeting training and development needs requires people to know what the learning objectives are and to have a clear, well-thought-through and well-supported plan or programme to meet them. It is not our intention in this book to describe how to put together a structured plan or programme; however, we will describe how competencies can contribute.

When structuring any training and development plan or programme using competencies, it is important to consider how progress will be monitored and evaluated. Factors that need to be considered when deciding on how progress is going to be measured include:

- What will be assessed? Will there be an assessment of knowledge, behaviour, skills, or a combination of some or all of these?
- How will skills, knowledge and behaviour be assessed? For example, skills and behaviour can be displayed only during the execution of a task or activity.
- How will objectivity be ensured?
- When will an individual be 'assessed'? Will this be at set times or when a certain level of skill is seen to have been achieved?
- Who will assess performance? Will it be the line manager, someone external to the team, or someone external to the company?
- How will consistency of assessment be assured?
- What will be the result of successful completion of each stage? Will there be a pay or grade increase?
- What will be the result of unsuccessful completion of a stage? Will there be remedial training and development? How many times can an individual redo a particular stage? How long can an individual be on the programme overall?

A competency framework will assist in the measurement of behaviours mentioned in the first two bullet points above.

An important issue to consider, when using competencies for the measurement of progress, is whether additional information is required. For example, if a competency framework has been designed for a whole organisation, the behavioural indicators will be in a generic form. Further information may therefore be needed to describe:

- the context in which the behaviours are to be demonstrated (for example – What exactly is the definition of 'the business' in the behaviour 'Seeks and promotes innovation to take the business forward'?)
- the limits that behaviours are not expected to exceed (for example – What customers would not be included in the behaviour 'Establishes customer information needs in order to communicate effectively with customers'?)

- the underlying knowledge that is required (for example – What would individuals need to know about before they could develop skills that demonstrate their competency in 'Uses appropriate planning to succeed in own role'?).

The points made so far are general to the structure of training and development plans and programmes. However, there are more specific issues that need to be addressed, depending on whether the training and development plans and programmes are meeting the needs of the:

- organisation
- profession
- individual.

Training and development programmes at organisation level

At an organisation level, training and development is focused on the progress of individuals to a skill level within an organisation rather than within a specific job. This is typical of:

- succession-planning programmes (such as management training programmes) through which long-term training and development needs are addressed
- change management programmes through which current shortfalls of skills are addressed.

With succession-planning programmes, the skills of a population are to be improved or increased without knowing exactly when those skills will be used, or in what part of the organisation. Time-frames for 'success' are usually fairly flexible, where they exist at all, and learning objectives tend to concentrate more on generic management competencies that have been identified as core throughout the business at a particular level rather than on competencies specific to a particular job.

Change management programmes will usually have shorter time-frames and have more specific learning objectives, because they will be addressing clearly identified current training and development needs.

Competencies can help structure an organisation-wide training and development programme because they describe the behaviours needed to meet the organisation's need – for example, if a change management programme has identified the need for improved customer service within an organisation. If readers are using our **Appendix Framework**, the required behaviours will be found in the GROWS BUSINESS CAPABILITY cluster, under the competency heading Customer Focus (see page 134). The training and development events and activities within the programme can then be selected to focus on achieving those behaviours.

Competency frameworks can also be used to structure longer-term training and development programmes – for example, where senior management roles within an organisation have been profiled (ie competencies for those roles have been identified), behaviours at levels identified as key for senior managers will provide the focus of longer-term development programmes for more junior managers. Role profiling is described in **Appendix 3**.

Designing programmes now to develop people for roles that they may not fulfil for many years raises some interesting issues. Recent research, reported by Kandola and Galpin (2002/03), suggests two key issues with using competencies for management development programmes:

- 'The role of a senior manager changes many times during their career, and taking account of these key points is absolutely critical in determining the outcome of the high-flier's journey.' Therefore, deciding early on in someone's career whether they have the capability to become a senior manager is very difficult to predict.

■ 'How can we be sure that what makes a successful high performer now will still apply in 10 or 15 years' time?'

In order to address these issues, Kandola and Galpin suggest that, by analysing the characteristics of successful individuals, a list of 'metacompetencies' can be drawn up. Quoting research done by McCall, Spreitzer and Mahoney (1994), Kandola and Galpin quote a number of factors that distinguish successful high-potential individuals from the rest:

■ seeks opportunities to learn
■ acts with integrity
■ adapts to cultural differences
■ is committed to making a difference
■ seeks broad business knowledge
■ brings out the best in people
■ sees things from new angles
■ has the courage to take risks
■ seeks and uses feedback
■ learns from mistakes
■ is open to criticism.

Kandola and Galpin suggest that 'these, in effect, become overriding or metacompetencies that can be checked at various stages of someone's career'. In order to meet both the short- and long-term needs of the organisation, they recommend that 'high-fliers should be selected and developed using shorter-term competences (sic), but should also be assessed against the metacompetencies that concentrate on their ability to learn, so they can adapt as the organisation and its competences (sic) change.'

In practice, many of the statements listed above are more like generic behavioural indicators than competencies and as such may already be included in generic competencies for managers. Isolating these behaviours, from a generic framework, for specific assessment may be one way of ensuring that the 'adaptability' of the trainee is assessed and monitored.

When structuring a training and development programme for the long term, the shorter-term training and development needs of the individual for their current job must be taken into account.

Conflict management

A government agency put in place a senior management training programme that included a requirement for participants to develop planning skills. The senior management planning competency included behaviours that were based on looking at the 'big picture' and meeting long-term objectives. However, many participants were in roles where the planning competency included behaviours that were based on looking at the detail of tasks and meeting shorter-term objectives.

To avoid what was clearly a potentially conflicting development need (especially where the participant had to develop skills to meet both competencies) the management training programme included activities such as the management of projects. This allowed the management trainee to clearly separate the development of appropriate planning behaviours for both their current job and their (hopefully!) future senior management role.

This mix of short-term and long-term needs requires the careful design and management of training and development programmes to ensure that behaviours required both now and in the future can be practised. A competency framework (and/or metacompetencies) can only provide a focus for activities on such programmes, as many other factors – not least the willingness of the individual and his or her manager to support such development – play an important part in the results of succession or management training programmes.

Training and development programmes within a profession

Training and development programmes within a profession are designed and controlled by bodies outside the organisation in which the individual is employed. Organisational competency frameworks are unlikely to be aligned with professional competency frameworks unless the organisation has done work to ensure this. However, professional competencies can still be useful.

Many professional bodies recognise that knowledge alone is not enough – how their members use that knowledge (ie how they behave) is also important. To this end, many professions prescribe behaviours, or competencies, that their members are expected to display. For example, the Chartered Institute of Personnel and Development (CIPD) expect their members to exhibit a mixture of 10 competencies including 'Analytical and intuitive/creative thinking' and 'Personal drive and effectiveness'.

If an organisation is going to include progression on a profession's training and development programme within an individual's training and development plan, it is important that learning objectives don't clash. It is not unusual for the culture within an organisation to demand behaviour from an individual contrary to that which is expected by the professional body to which they belong. For example, pressure put on personnel managers to recruit people into the organisation in a way which would contravene the CIPD's best practice would create a conflict between actual behaviour and expected behaviour (as outlined in the CIPD's competency 'Professional and ethical behaviour').

While such situations may be a matter for the professional to deal with, it is worth considering these potential conflicts. How will a development programme that contains learning objectives built around behaviours that contradict a professional code of conduct be managed by the organisation? As stated earlier, a well-designed framework will reflect the behaviours required for good practice – so this conflict should be avoided with a competency framework that meets the performance standards described in Chapter 2 (**A Typical Competency Framework**).

For a profession, the design of a programme to train and develop their members in key behaviours is challenging, to say the least! Often, although there is control over the training element (in that courses and other events are endorsed by the profession), development events and activities are less easy to control. To date, many professions still structure their training and development programmes around knowledge. However, as more attention is given to the behavioural aspect of professional status, professional bodies will have to consider how to increase the focus on behaviour within their training and development programmes.

Training and development plans at individual level

The training and development plan for an individual may be based on the need to develop skills for their own job, or to meet the demands of an organisation's or profession's training and development programme. Either way, the person who is developing their skills should have a training and development plan that identifies their learning objectives. The learning objectives should be agreed with the individual before any training or development takes place.

For behavioural training and development needs, based on either aspirational behaviours or those required for the current job, a competency framework can assist in drawing up learning objectives. The behavioural indicators describing the competency that needs to be developed will help the individual and the line manager focus on what they expect to be different when learning has successfully taken place.

For example, if an individual has a need to learn some customer service techniques for 'GROWS BUSINESS CAPABILITY: Customer Focus, Level 2' (see page 134) of our **Appendix Framework**, the learning objectives will include one or more of the behaviours of Level 2. These are:

- seeks feedback from customers to enhance services and/or products
- responds appropriately to customer requests
- establishes customer information needs in order to communicate effectively with customers.

Table 22 shows an example of learning objectives and an action plan in this case.

Table 22 *Example of learning objectives and action plan*

Learning objectives for Chris Smith – Customer service

Learning objectives
- to enhance customer services through the use of customer feedback
- to respond appropriately to customer requests
- to communicate effectively with customers.

Action plan
- attend customer service techniques workshop by end of June
- attend workshop on how to use the customer feedback process by end of July
- work alongside team leader to develop telephone skills
- invite team leader to attend at least three customer meetings with you over the next two months for support and feedback
- meet with line manager once a fortnight for support and to discuss progress
- update line manager on how you have used information from the customer feedback process to improve customer service by the end of October.

Success criteria
- improvement in customer satisfaction survey results
- no justified complaints from customers.

With an agreed competency profile for the job (see **Appendix 3**), the training and development plan should aim to ensure that individuals have the necessary techniques and development opportunities to demonstrate the required behaviours. This means that development activities must allow the knowledge and techniques learned to be practised in a variety of appropriate situations. Activities are therefore likely to include a range of methods such as on-the-job coaching and simulations.

Once the action plan has been agreed, it needs to be implemented. How events are designed to meet needs, and how events are evaluated, is covered in later sections of this chapter.

Designing training and development events

Once a structured training and development plan or programme has been designed, events and activities need to be designed to meet the learning objectives the plan or programme is designed to address.

Training events contain activities in which an individual learns something new. Development events contain activities in which learning is put into practice in such a way as to develop skill and expertise. Training and development events can be highly structured (eg a training course or development centre) or informal (eg on-the-job activities). Table 23 illustrates what some of these events might be, together with some examples of activities. An event is likely to include, or be followed by, activities. An activity, however, does not have to be instigated or preceded by an event.

While there are many different ways of designing training and development events, designers usually have to take into account:

- the learning objectives of the participants, team, department and/or organisation
- current competency levels of the participants
- situation(s) in which the learning will be put into practice
- available training expertise – internally or externally
- available resources (eg money, time, materials and space).

With the exception of the available resources, competency frameworks can help in all of these considerations.

Table 23 *Examples of training and development events and activities*

Training events	Development events	Activities
■ courses/classes ■ seminars ■ lectures ■ workshops ■ distance learning ■ on-the-job training (taking instruction while doing the job)	■ development centres ■ team-building workshops ■ skills practice events ■ rehearsals	■ trying something different ■ observation of, or discussions with, a more experienced person ■ project work ■ secondments to another area ■ simulation exercises/assignments ■ team-building exercises

Learning objectives

The successful outcome of any training event should be:

- in the short term that the individuals gained the knowledge and/or techniques they were supposed to learn about (ie the event achieved its objectives)
- in the longer term that the individuals successfully put the knowledge and/or techniques into practice through skills developed while doing development activities (ie the individuals achieve their learning objectives).

The objectives of a well-designed training or development event will take into account learning objectives. People do not usually attend events just to learn a particular technique or acquire particular knowledge for the sake of it. They need the techniques or knowledge in order to achieve something else. For example, the learning objective for someone attending a planning course is to learn planning techniques that they can then apply in their job to become more organised or manage projects more efficiently. Many events fail because their designers have not considered the context in which the learner will be applying new knowledge or new techniques.

Running out of time

A major financial institution was running training in telephone techniques for its customer service staff. The course focused on the customer service element of the calls. However, the customer service objectives of the training were never fully met because the event neglected to train these techniques in the high-pressure, high-turnaround requirements of the real day-to-day situation. Staff simply didn't have time to ask customers if they had fully understood what had just been said, or to ask if there was anything else they could help the customer with, because they were under pressure to answer as many calls in each hour as they could.

Organisations will arrange training and development events to meet identified needs. Competency frameworks will inform the general learning objectives of these events as they describe effective behaviours needed at certain levels of competency. For example, if there is a requirement to improve team leadership in an organisation, the competency framework will indicate what effective team leadership should look like.

Development events and activities also need to take into account the learning objectives of the participant. Those delivering or supporting the event/activity need to understand the behaviours that the participant is seeking to improve to ensure that their input is valuable. As we have mentioned earlier in this chapter, development of skills assumes that the person has the required knowledge and/or techniques. If they don't, they will need to be trained first.

Current competency level of participants

Although an event is designed to meet certain learning objectives, the current competency level of participants will help structure the material. Material that is too complex or too simple will quickly 'turn off' participants, however well it is presented.

Methods for finding out the competency levels of event participants include:

- pre-event questionnaires for participants and/or line managers
- performance ratings

- a review of training records
- personal knowledge of participants.

Competency frameworks can assist in finding out current levels of competency, mostly by providing a framework for pre-event questionnaires.

One of the primary purposes of a pre-event questionnaire should be to establish the level of training or development a participant has already had. The questionnaire is likely to include questions about the participant's knowledge and experience, and a questionnaire can focus on the competencies to be covered by the event. For example, an adapted version of the audit questionnaire in Table 21 could be used.

The results of this questionnaire can give the person who is delivering the event a feel for where to concentrate his or her efforts. It may be that one or two particular behaviours are causing problems – and these may be different for each group of participants on the course.

Other information may be requested, such as previous training in a similar area, development activities already undertaken, and so on. However, remember that long and complex questionnaires have a lower return rate than short, straightforward ones.

Another source of information could be the results from a formal performance review. Performance ratings based only on outputs are not particularly helpful because a low score could have been given for a number of reasons. Performance ratings that include a review of competencies (as discussed in Chapter 5 – **Using Competencies to Review Performance**) are more helpful. For example, a low score in sales achievement coupled with a low score in influencing could give the trainer useful insights – reviewers' comments could be very useful if confidentiality is not an issue.

Multi-rater performance reviews, as outlined in Chapter 5 (**Using Competencies to Review Performance**), can also provide useful insights. For example, it may be that direct reports tend to see a different side of their manager's 'leadership style' from that seen by the manager's colleagues. This information can be used to focus the training more accurately on the need.

Performance review ratings alone are often not the most accurate measures of competency, especially where they are linked to pay reviews. Frankness about training and development needs in an interview, when the outcome will directly affect a person's pay, is not guaranteed! There will also be confidentiality issues to consider. It is better, for training and development purposes, either to use another measure (eg the outcome of an assessment process) or to supplement the performance review rating with other information.

Training records may give the trainer insight into the techniques and knowledge a person should have, but participation in a training event does not guarantee learning or application of learning. However, training records will give useful information about whether to include 'refresher' sessions or to start from scratch.

Personal knowledge of the candidates may help a trainer prepare for the delivery of an event. This is most likely where the trainer is already part of a team (eg as the line manager). However, there is the danger that assumptions might be made in place of exploring facts. The competency framework can, again, be a useful structure to explore areas of training and development needs to help focus the learning and the teaching on key behaviours. This could be done through the methods outlined above. For example: if a whole team is attending an event, a pre-event questionnaire could be used; if an individual is attending an event, an informal discussion could be structured around the competency framework.

All methods for finding out the current competency level of participants have potential flaws, and therefore the more careful and thorough the information-collecting, the better.

Situations in which the learning could be put into practice

The best training and development events and activities are those that relate to actual situations in which the participant needs to use their skills. How many times have individuals sat in courses, seminars and so on and thought 'This is all very well, but it's not like this where I work'? It is not an easy task for a trainer to replicate the workplace exactly because it is rare that any two situations are exactly the same. However, the closer the link to 'reality' the better.

The right chemistry!

A staff satisfaction survey in a multinational oil and chemicals company revealed concerns regarding the way staff felt they were being managed. One option would have been to teach individuals how to manage through some form of standardised training programme. However, it would have been very difficult to account for the different circumstances in which people-management skills were required and the different levels of ability to be found in managers attending the programme.

It was decided to produce a development workshop that would provide supervisors and managers with an opportunity to be observed and get feedback while they managed people. Benchmarks for the workshop were five people-management competencies. Activities in the workshop were simulations of common situations in which people-management competencies would be found within the organisation – for example, appraisals, project management and a meeting to communicate change to a team. Actors were used to play the team members of the supervisors and managers.

The workshop design ensured that each individual manager's people-management issues were identified and discussed in terms of further development. The programme, although common to all managers, was therefore able to address each individual manager's needs.

Although some managers and supervisors thought they would not gain from 'training in people management', all managers attending the workshop (over 200 supervisors and managers worldwide) praised its relevance and usefulness. The most cited reasons for this feedback were 'the realism of the simulations' and 'the quality of feedback from the actors and observers'.

A competency framework can help to ensure that training and development events are realistic. Behaviours drawn from situations encountered in the organisation, department, business unit and so on will reflect what is happening in that organisation. Those designing a training or development event will then have ready-made guidance in the design of simulation exercises.

To illustrate this point we refer back to our **Appendix Framework**. A training workshop designed to help managers improve their personal planning skills relates to the 'SHOWS THE WAY: Planning' competency at Level 3 (see page 133). The behaviours outlined in this competency are:

- sets SMART objectives for self and/or team
- regularly reviews progress of plans to redirect action when necessary
- considers 'what ifs' and uses contingency plans to minimise risks

- plans activities based on the needs of those who will be affected by them.

We therefore know that any simulation exercises should ensure that the managers get the opportunity to:

- identify and set clear objectives
- decide when a plan has to change, and when it doesn't
- review and adapt plans to redirect action when necessary
- identify risks
- consider 'what ifs' and use contingency plans to minimise risks
- find out the needs of others and take those needs into account when planning.

Exercises with these behaviours in mind will relate to reality because these behaviours come from reality.

It is important, however, not to rely just on the competency framework for context information. Each team will be facing different scenarios, and good training and development events will take account of the current situation in a team, upcoming changes (to procedures or to the structure of the organisation), and so on.

It is worth mentioning development centres here. We feel there is an important distinction between centres that are designed to assess an individual's competency against a predetermined benchmark, and centres that give an individual the opportunity to practise techniques. The first type of centre is an assessment process in which marks are often allocated and action plans for development are often directed at a specific role or group of roles. Such assessment-for-development centres (ADCs) are similar in design to assessment centres for selection, but differ in terms of the number of competencies covered, the feedback (which is more wide-ranging), and the outcome (no participant is actually selected at that stage). These differences also mean that the brief for the centre's assessors will be different, as their role is more that of a facilitator/coach. ADCs are covered in Chapter 5 – **Using Competencies to Review Performance**.

The second type of centre, a development centre (DC), has a purely developmental focus. It is a realistic work simulation in which the participant's behaviour is observed and in which opportunities are provided for skills development – as illustrated in our example, **The right chemistry**.

Development centres are increasing in popularity, particularly for senior management development. A typical senior management DC is run over one to three days and will include:

- 'real' meetings, usually with professional actors briefed to explore specific issues
- realistic flows of information – eg through the use of e-mails, diaries and in-trays
- working from a 'real' office
- learning sessions where managers practice skills in specific areas of need with fully briefed actors and/or facilitators.

Such realistic situations allow participants to try out new techniques and hone existing skills in a safe environment. They also allow participants to use all their skills in a 'joined-up' way – rather than go through exercises in which they only focus on one competency at a time.

Playing out the role!

A business services consultancy was preparing its successful consultants for more senior roles. Over a two-and-a-half-day period the consultants were 'put into' more senior roles – with their clients, colleagues and team members played by actors. During this time, the consultants fulfilled diary commitments, met with colleagues and clients etc, and responded to emails while being observed by highly skilled coaches.

After each meeting, consultants were asked to use the competencies for the more senior role to review how the meeting went. Consultants were also given feedback by the actor (in the role of client, colleague, etc) and by the coach. Over the two and a half days the consultants were able to build up a picture of their strengths and development needs for the more senior role.

Each consultant discussed and compared their views of strengths and development needs with their coach. Training and development priorities were discussed, and where new knowledge or new techniques were needed, then training was provided. Where techniques were understood, but poorly used, a practice session was planned with an actor to help develop skills in using the technique(s). Longer-term development plans would then be agreed between the consultants and their managers.

Performance is not rated; rather, participants are encouraged to reflect on what they did, helped by getting good feedback from facilitators and actors. Learning points and action plans from such development centres are directed to further development within each individual's current role, or one for which he or she has already been selected or is aspiring to.

Available training expertise

Not all trainers are able to deliver all training events. Not all managers are skilful enough to support all development activities. Competencies could be linked to a system which identifies who can do what in the way of delivery and/or support. For example, more senior managers and executives are making use of coaching and mentoring services. Being a coach or mentor in these circumstances may require a higher level of 'influencing' than running events with more junior staff and are likely to require a higher level of 'managing relationships' than those involving more straightforward support.

Categorising competencies needed for particular events or activities may work well for a training department, which may be linking competency to progression anyway. However, it is likely to be a much more complex task across a whole organisation.

If external trainers, coaches or mentors are used, it is important that they are familiar with the competency framework in use in the organisation. They need to know what behaviours are key in the organisation and the roles within which their trainees or 'mentees' are working, and also need to be using the same language when talking about behaviours.

Selecting appropriate training and development events or activities

Once a training and/or development need has been identified, either for a specific job, or as part of a programme, an appropriate way of meeting that need has to be found. Training needs are more likely to be met through formal training events – development needs through informal development activities. There are several ways in which suitable events are made public (eg directories of training courses), but development activities are often less well communicated.

Competency frameworks can be used to identify suitable activities by matching events and activities against each competency level and even against behavioural indicators. An increasingly popular way of doing this is by producing a development directory. Table 24 is an example page of a fictional directory based on our **Appendix Framework**.

Competency frameworks are often used as the structure for these directories. Development activities and resources can be organised using the competency, the competency level or the behavioural indicators. In Table 24, where resources are organised by competency level, there is mention of a video called *On Being a Team Member*. This may not, at first glance, seem to fit with a development need for 'planning'. However, one of the behaviours in Planning, Level 3, is 'Plans activities based on the needs of those who will be affected by them' (see page 133). The second section of this video may help to highlight the impact on the members of one's team of not planning one's daily tasks properly.

Table 24 *Example of events and activities to meet training and development need(s)*

SHOWS THE WAY: Planning
Level 3: Uses appropriate planning to succeed in own role

Suggested training events:

How to make use of a diary	workshop	½ day on-site
Objective-setting	workshop	½ day on-site
Time management	course	2 days off-site
Planning techniques	course	2 days off-site
How to prioritise	distance learning course (video and workbook)	estimated 5 hours
Priorities, Priorities	video	1½ hours

Suggested development events and activities:
Note: You may find it helpful to undertake these activities with the knowledge and support of your line manager. Set timescales for reviewing progress. Discuss the outcomes with your line manager and agree follow-up actions if needed.

- Use a diary or time-planner to schedule future plans.
- Use a 'To Do' list for daily tasks.
- Watch Section 2 of the video *On Being a Team Member* (takes about 1 hour). Consider the impact of your actions on others, and think of any appropriate action you can take to minimise the possibility of negative impact on others resulting from your actions.
- Make estimates at the start of each day of how far through your work you think you will be at certain times (eg mid-morning, lunch, mid-afternoon). Compare this with your actual progress, and reflect on any differences.
- Think about the 'what ifs' of a situation and what you will do if those circumstances arise. Talk to others who have done similar tasks to see what the likely pitfalls are. Check back to see how the situation went, and how useful your contingency plans were. Adjust future plans to benefit from your learning.

Drawing up such a directory is clearly a time-consuming task if it is to be comprehensive. It also requires constant maintenance to ensure that it remains valid. However, many companies now use technology for drafting, and even communicating and managing, training and development directories, making life easier for all concerned.

'Plugging' into the system

A paper-based development directory was produced for a life assurance company. It was very popular with sales staff, for whom it was designed, and other staff wanted something similar. This resulted in a number of directories, each of which required reprinting and redistribution when adapted and/or updated.

Many of the activities in the different directories were similar, and of course core competencies were repeated in each directory. So a single directory was produced to cover all jobs. This single directory took existing directories and 'plugged' them straight into a specially developed computer package. Updating and distribution is now much easier.

The computer package also provides much greater flexibility because it can in turn have any new directories 'plugged' into it and can be linked to computer-based performance reviews. This enables reviewers to go through the full process of collecting and reviewing behavioural feedback and then establishing development events and activities to address development needs.

Exactly which event or activity to choose will depend on the environmental and individual factors that influence training and development mentioned at the beginning of this chapter.

Evaluating the success of training and development

As already stated, any training and development plan or programme should have clearly identified learning objectives. These objectives will contain measures such as timescales and success criteria (ie what the learning is aiming to achieve). How successful the plan or programme has been, or is being, in meeting these objectives requires the assessment of individuals' achievements against the learning objectives outlined in the plan or programme.

There are two important aspects of training and development to evaluate. The first is whether events and activities meet the learning objectives of the individual. The second is whether the combination of events and activities within training and development programmes meet the learning objectives of an organisation or profession.

Within this section we look at how organisations can use competencies to:

- evaluate training and development activities and events
- evaluate training and development programmes.

Evaluating training and development activities and events
As outlined earlier, the successful outcomes of training or development events should be to meet learning objectives.

Evaluating the success of training and development has caused organisations many headaches, not least because it is difficult to know whether any improvement in skills is down to an activity or event or to circumstances that would have happened anyway – particularly when measuring across a large number of people. For example, was last month's increase in profits a result of the customer services training or of the article in a daily newspaper that showed our product as one of the best?

We are not suggesting that measuring the worth of the event or activity is a waste of time. It is prudent to ensure that the time and effort an organisation puts into training and development is well spent. Competencies aid the evaluation process because they describe the effective behaviours against which an individual can be compared – and if there is a positive change of behaviour following training and development, it would not be unreasonable to suggest that the investment was successful.

Assessing how successful an event has been in achieving its objectives is reasonably straightforward – provided that the event had clear objectives, of course. Traditionally, this sort of evaluation has been effected through a questionnaire given out at the end of an event. However, it is widely acknowledged that this is not the best method of evaluating whether any learning has actually taken place.

Another way of assessing achievement of event objectives is to ask participants to take a test. For example, many professional courses end with exams, the results of which are often used to assess the success of the course itself.

Although this sort of evaluation may yield useful information about the event itself, it is a mistake to translate this to the success (or otherwise) of the learning.

Course not

A personnel officer was sent on a job-analysis course to learn how to analyse jobs. There was an end-of-course assessment that she passed with flying colours.

She was not required to do any job analysis in the workplace until six months after the course. Not surprisingly, in this case the attendance on the course did not translate to skill-in-job analysis!

A more relevant evaluation of the worth of training time and effort is that of the success of participants in achieving their learning objectives. This, as with the evaluation of events, assumes that such objectives have been agreed.

At an appropriate time after the event, achievement of learning objectives should be assessed. By focusing on behaviours, not only is the learning of information and techniques assessed, but also whether these are making the required difference. To use the example given in Table 22 earlier, did Chris learn how to use the customer feedback process (ie did the training work?) and has Chris's behaviour changed (ie did the development work?)?

Guidelines on how to measure learning objectives need to be developed and agreed with assessors. These guidelines should cover such issues as:

- what evidence is acceptable (eg records of achievement, copies of written work produced, random checks on telephone calls with customers)
- how many times an individual must demonstrate a behaviour before being considered effective

- how evidence can be produced where opportunities to demonstrate a particular behaviour are infrequent.

These guidelines must be available to the participants in the programme as well as to the assessors. It is advisable that how an individual is to be assessed is made clear before the asssessment takes place. Even in situations where there are to be spot checks it should be made clear that these will happen over a specified period of time. Without such openness there is a danger that the programme becomes seen as a 'spying' process, and rumours will develop about the true purpose of the assessment.

Deciding who should collect such evaluation information is an important consideration. At line manager or department level, 'global' information is lost. At a central point, 'local' information is lost. A good system ensures that managers are responsible for the collection of the information (after all, they are the ones who are in the best position to feed back the success of the learning and it is in their interests to know how successful it has been) and that a central point (usually the training department) is responsible for collating the results. This way, not only can the managers keep track of the investment of time and effort of themselves and their team members, but the organisation can ensure that training and development events are achieving the learning that the strategy requires.

Central collection of training data can also be used to identify available skills within an organisation.

Who's there?

A large consultancy company found that as they grew it became increasingly difficult to know who was skilled in what areas. They therefore set up a skills database from which they could identify three types of consultant: those who could head up projects; those who could support them; and those who had an interest in developing skills in key areas. Using this database in conjunction with the office diary, projects could be resourced to not only maximise the current skills of the consultants, but also to expose developing consultants to projects that would enhance their skills for the future.

Low evaluation results may not mean that the event was poor – it may mean that there is another training need or that the action plan was not adhered to. With learning objectives using behavioural statements, such as those illustrated in Table 22, it can be decided whether the effort of the event was worthwhile (ie did Chris meet the objectives?).

In our experience, despite an organisation's desire for money allocated to training to be well spent, one of the main reasons that successful training events don't translate into skilful employees is that there is insufficient support when the trainee undertakes development activities. Line managers are key in helping their staff apply training through allocating appropriate tasks and resources, and supporting them whilst skills develop. This is one of the reasons we recommend that learning objectives are discussed before training takes place, to ensure that a plan will be in place for after the event. Organisations can also be at fault here, because they don't factor any, or enough, 'practice time' into their headcount to allow skills to develop.

Evaluating training and development programmes
Evaluating the success of training and development events concentrates on the outcomes of individual events. When these events are combined in a programme to meet organisational or professional objectives, the effectiveness of that programme needs to be assessed.

There are four key differences between evaluating an event and a programme:

- timescales
- the number of competencies being assessed
- the implications of the outcomes
- the evaluation of learning for future or professional roles.

Evaluation of a programme is likely to be at one or more key stages throughout the programme, usually identified at the outset. For example, it may be at fixed intervals (eg every year throughout a management training programme) or at the conclusion of a particular initiative (eg six months after a change management programme concluded).

It is often the case that programmes will require progress on a number of competencies. For example, a management training programme will usually include development on a range of key management competencies. Evaluation of progress on a programme is always best measured through assessment of how the individual behaves in the most realistic situation. For many this will be in the job they are doing. However, we still see organisations use assessment-for-development centres (ADCs) to measure progress, despite there being ample evidence available from the participant's job. ADCs, to monitor progress, should only be necessary where the job for which participants are developing their skills requires a different level of competency, or a significantly different environment, from the job they currently hold.

Although success on the training and development programme should be the key aim of everyone involved, it should be made clear to participants what the results of failure will be. For example, if a trainee's continued employment depends on successful completion of the programme, it should be made clear at the outset.

Assessment of individual progress, particularly in job- or salary-rise-dependent programmes, must be objective and fair. This is not only so that the organisation focuses its efforts correctly, but also to avoid accusations of unfair treatment – eg unfair treatment because of the team that people work in or the manager they work for. Using a competency framework, especially one that has already been established, as the benchmark against which progress is measured is a good way of achieving objectivity.

Measuring progress in training and development programmes is often overlaid with progress within a particular job. For example, if the programme involves stints of a particular length of time in various departments, the trainee may well have specific learning objectives during each stint as well as learning objectives within the management training programme itself. It is important that there is clarity about who is supporting and measuring what objectives, and how the objectives are to be achieved. Without this clarity there is potential for conflict between development for the long term and development in the short term.

Managing to do better

A multinational corporation identified a need, through a staff satisfaction survey, to improve the quality of support that staff receive from their managers. A training and development programme was put in place and over 100 managers went through the programme during one year.

The programme was evaluated in two ways. The specific training and development issues of each manager were identified and collated during the programme. This was followed up with one-to-one interviews with the managers, three to six months after the programme, to find out if they were doing things differently regarding their identified needs. The second evaluation was a re-run of the original staff satisfaction survey, to see if there had been an improvement in the overall rating on staff management.

Both evaluations confirmed that the programme had achieved its objectives.

Measuring progression within professional training and development programmes is not easy when it comes to assessing behaviours. To date, there is still a heavy reliance on exams, tests and coursework to evaluate the success of such programmes. However, with an increased demand from many professional bodies that their members must provide evidence of continuous professional development, progress can be monitored through the type of evidence collected – for example, witness statements forming part of a record of achievement. These witness statements could be explicitly related to the competencies for which the programme was designed, eg examples of the trainee's use of specified competencies.

As mentioned in the previous section, deciding who should collect evaluation information is an important consideration. Line managers are best placed to collect evidence of progress within a job. Properly trained assessors will collect evidence if more formal assessment events are used. However the information is collected, it must be collated in order to assess how well the learning objectives of the programme are being met.

KEY POINTS

- Two key purposes for training and development are to ensure that the competencies of staff are sufficient to meet both current and future needs.
- A wide range of factors influence not only what training and development events and activities are offered by an organisation, but also how much actual learning takes place.
- Organisational strategic plans and policies will affect what training and development is on offer.
- Environmental factors, especially the culture of the organisation, and individual factors such as learning style, motivation and abilities, will affect how much individuals actually learn.
- Training is about the teaching of information and techniques.
- Development is about using information and techniques in a focused and supported manner, resulting in skill and expertise.
- Training events that are not followed up with development activities result in the learning soon being forgotten.
- Development activities undertaken in ignorance of the information and/or techniques required for their success will result in errors.

- Competency frameworks provide examples of effective behaviour that inform the:
  - benchmarks against which performance is compared when identifying training and development needs and when evaluating the success of plans and programmes designed to address them
  - structuring, design and selection of events and activities that can focus on providing information and/or techniques and practice situations to achieve these behaviours.

- The use of a competency framework will improve training and development within an organisation, but without skilled people to design, deliver and support the events and activities, competency-based training and development will be no better than any other poorly resourced process.

REFERENCES AND READING

KANDOLA B. and GALPIN M. (2002/03) 'Assessing and developing high-fliers: the case for meta-competencies'. *Competency & Emotional Intelligence*. Vol. 10, No.2, Winter 2002/03. pp20–24.

McCALL M, SPREITZER G and MAHONEY J. (1994) *Identifying leadership potential in future international executives: a learning resource guide*. Lexington, MA, International Consortium for Executive Development Research.

Using competencies to support pay and grading

Since the first edition of this book there has been an increased use of competency frameworks for most people-management functions. However, this does not seem to be the case for pay and grading. Indeed, there is evidence that competency-related pay is becoming less popular, not more (*Competency & Emotional Intelligence*, 2002). This is perhaps not surprising when there is little evidence that linking competencies directly with pay and grading shows any reported increase in output or job satisfaction – although this may be more to do with the way such schemes are implemented than the principles of linking competencies to pay. However, there is clearly some link in most organisations between the performance of an individual, the grade they occupy and their financial rewards. As many organisations use competencies for performance management, and link performance into pay, we have kept this chapter in this second edition.

Pay and grading are most often linked when job grades set limits for the rewards available to a job-holder. The job-holder's job performance determines what pay he or she will receive within the grade limits. Even in organisations where there is no formal performance-related pay system, in almost all cases pay and performance will be linked in some way.

In this chapter 'pay' refers to the financial rewards individuals receive for their work and therefore includes variable and 'one-off' rewards, such as bonuses and commission as well as salary and wages. 'Grading' refers to structures that distinguish between jobs on the basis of perceived value, levels of responsibility and other job characteristics that make up jobs in an organisation. The reward structure is usually overlaid on the grading structure to indicate the range of reward for ranges of job grades. Rules for variable financial rewards are usually established within a company policy or procedure.

THE PURPOSE OF PAY AND GRADING

A pay structure may have many and varied purposes. However, the key purposes include:

- motivation
- rewarding performance fairly
- the retention and attraction of staff
- recognition of achievement
- confirmation and support of the organisation's culture.

The purposes of grading structures also vary – between organisations – but are likely to include:

- setting pay bands – within market rates or not
- assisting in management of the pay budget
- recognition of value/job worth – internally
- recognition of value/job worth – externally
- providing motivation for development
- providing a structure for succession.

A pay structure, when linked to a grading structure, may well have overlapping minimum and maximum levels – that is, the maximum salary of one grade may be more than the minimum salary of the next grade. This allows for the means of recognising that experienced people, performing to a high standard, are more valuable to an organisation, at least in the short term, than a trainee on the next grade. Organisations may also decide to fix a point around which an individual who is able to do the job, and does so to an acceptable level of performance, is paid. Above this point are paid high-performers and more experienced individuals; below this point are paid low-performers or trainees.

Colourful rewards

A major finance company subdivides its job grades into colour zones. In each job grade there is a blue zone based on the level of competency expected of a trainee. The next colour zone is amber, which indicates the level of competency for minimum effective performance within the job. Finally, there is a red zone which describes the level of competency that would be observed of individuals contributing above the minimum effective level.

The pay bands for job grades are divided into these three zones. Individuals therefore know the range of pay they are likely to receive, depending on their level of competency. In addition, the zones provide some indication of, and motivation for, development of competencies required in the job.

Figure 4 shows how this type of pay and grading system might look. It is not unusual for this sort of system to have wider and more overlapping bands for more senior grades. There is often a wider range of jobs that fit into these grades with the requirement for a wide range of salaries.

Whatever grading system is used, in order that jobs can be positioned in it some form of evaluation mechanism is employed. Where grading is linked to pay, evaluation systems attempt to identify the worth of a job to an organisation in order that the individual who holds that job can be remunerated correctly. Competencies can help in the evaluation process by contributing to the assessment of what is important in a job. The factors governing what 'correct' remuneration means varies between sectors, professions and organisations, and even within organisations.

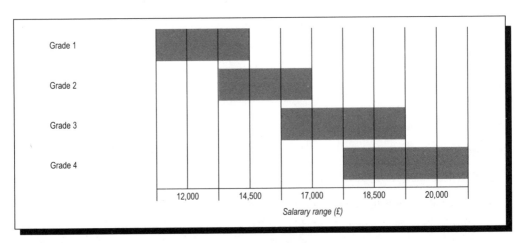

Figure 4 *Example of a pay and grading system with overlapping salary bands*

EFFECTIVE PAY AND GRADING SYSTEMS

The factors that influence the pay policy and structure in an organisation vary, depending on what system that organisation has put in place. However, all structures are likely to consider:

- the contribution of the individual
- the value of the individual to the organisation
- the scarcity of potential job-holders
- time served in the company and/or job
- the cost of living
- the financial position of the organisation
- other benefits and bonuses making up an overall remuneration package
- the frequency of pay reviews
- how quickly changes may be needed to respond to market pressures
- the success (or otherwise) of the organisation
- agreements with unions, staff associations, etc
- legal regulations.

The factors that influence the grading policy and structure are likely to include:

- the contribution to the organisation of work outputs
- the organisational structure
- the organisation's size
- external benchmarking
- the job evaluation system/policy.

Combining these factors, when considering an integrated pay and grading structure, shows that the area is a complex one.

USING COMPETENCIES IN PAY AND GRADING

As mentioned above, when pay and grading structures are linked there has to be some way of identifying:

- which grade a certain job belongs to
- how much pay, within a set band, an individual should receive for the job he or she does.

We will look at each of these factors separately.

Grading structures

Most job evaluation systems fall into one of three categories:

- *Individual negotiation* – where each job-holder is 'graded' on his or her specific skills, abilities, etc. In effect this is unlikely to result in grades as such, because it is the person who holds the job that is evaluated as much as the job itself. This sort of system is typical of the professional sports and entertainment industries.
- *Whole-job ranking* – comparing the value of a job within an organisation with the value of other

jobs. This approach is not analytical in that the detail or component parts of a job are not analysed separately; instead, the job is considered as a whole.

■ *Factor comparisons* – where component parts of a job are analysed and 'marks' are given in relation to the relative worth of each factor. Marks are added up and an overall score for the job is calculated.

Each of these systems requires a valuation of what is important to the organisation – ie the features of a job that make it worth more, or less, than other jobs. In the past these features have often been the size of the budget, the complexity of the decisions being made by the job-holder, the number of staff being managed, the knowledge required to undertake the job, and so on. Most of these features are outputs or tasks: the 'what' of the job. Some organisations are now introducing inputs, the 'how' of the job, into job evaluation and grading, and this is where competencies start to feature.

In an integrated competency approach, it makes sense to include the factors that are considered key in recruitment, training, development and performance management into the job evaluation and grading systems. This is not a straightforward process, because grading is about jobs rather than performance. However, the key way in which competency frameworks can assist in the grading process is by adding an extra element to the question, 'What is valued in this organisation?' – ie what features make one job worth more, or less, than another?

When jobs are being analysed for evaluation purposes, it is to investigate the features already deemed important to an organisation. If a competency framework exists for that organisation, it is not unreasonable for the level of competency required to do that job to be taken into account. However, there does seem to be a need for some caution to be exercised. Although many competency frameworks are split into levels, this is rarely done solely on the basis of job grade. So although there may be a relationship between the job level within the organisation and the competency level required to undertake that job, it is not always so.

We warned against the use of grades to indicate competency levels in Chapter 2 (**A Typical Competency Framework**). The same, in reverse, can be said in this section. It is unlikely to be appropriate to use competency levels to set grading structures. This is because the competency framework is designed to show different levels, within each competency, of behaviour. Some competencies may have a different number of levels from others. The same job may require a different level of each competency.

Figure 5 illustrates the different levels of competency in a generic framework with nine competencies (not the **Appendix Framework** used in this book). It would be difficult to tie the levels of this framework to grades, because not all competencies consist of the same number of levels. So, for example, it would not be possible to say that all senior management jobs were at Level 4 because only two competencies go up to that level.

Figures 6 and 7 show two job profiles overlaid on the generic framework. The first is a junior job, the second a more senior one. The shaded areas indicate the competency levels required.

In neither of the two examples do the jobs require all competencies at the same level. We can also see that the job in Example 2 (Figure 7) actually requires a 'lower' level of competency 5 than the more junior job. To tie competency levels directly in with grades in these circumstances would require extensive manipulation of either the competency framework or the grading system. Neither option is really workable.

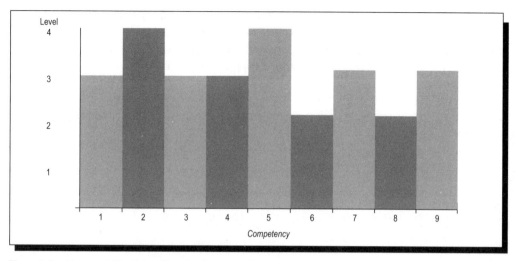

Figure 5 *Graphic presentation of competency levels in a core framework*

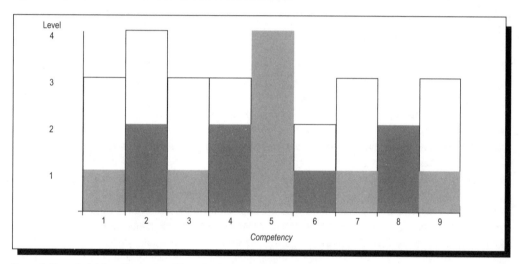

Figure 6 *Example 1: job profile showing different levels of competency required*

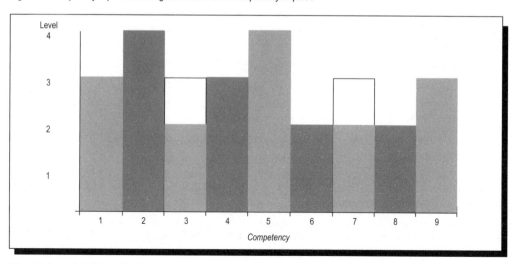

Figure 7 *Example 2: job profile showing different levels of competency required*

A more thorough integration of competency frameworks into grading structures is to account for competency levels along with other job features – for example, by allocating 'marks' to the various competency levels and combining these marks with the scores obtained by rating other features. This may seem reasonably straightforward, but it raises a number of issues such as:

- How many 'marks' would the different levels be awarded?
- Are all competencies to be rated as equal – or are some more valuable than others and therefore worthy of a weighting?
- Could the same competency/level be valued differently in different jobs?
- Where are the benchmarks for comparison going to come from?

Whilst this process will involve a lot of data-gathering and analysis, once completed a comprehensive, tailored job evaluation system will be possible.

For 'marks' to be allocated to competency levels, behaviours can be used to help structure the considerations of job evaluation committees on the relative worth of specific competency levels. For example, the competency 'SHOWS THE WAY: Planning, Level 2, Ensures plans meet local needs and that they account for the needs of other teams' (see page 133) in our **Appendix Framework** has the following behavioural indicators:

- Highlights key milestones and celebrates success in reaching them
- Works within and across business functions to plan and achieve objectives
- Ensures plans are compatible with wider business goals.

A job evaluation committee might consider each of these example behaviours to help build their estimate of the relative value that 'Ensuring plans meet local needs and that they account for the needs of other teams' gives to the organisation.

The point here is to establish a value for the contribution of the competency or competency level to the overall value of the job. Therefore, care should be taken to avoid double counting, ie take care to stay focused on competency behaviours and not the job activities or outputs that the behaviours might be used to achieve. The job activities and outputs may already be used as evaluation factors.

Once jobs are evaluated, they have to be matched against an agreed grading system. The grading systems that organisations use vary enormously. Grading systems can be based on:

- straightforward hierarchies – eg grades 1–10, with 1 the most junior and 10 the most senior
- various types of job – eg management, technical, clerical, executive
- levels within grades – eg four different levels within each grade (so a job might be Grade 1 but there might be a trainee, application, expert and coach level)
- roles – eg researchers, consultants, senior consultants and partners in a professional organisation.

Organisations may have a number of different grading systems in place to take account of different needs within different parts of the business.

Where competencies have been brought into pay and grading, the most common application appears to be in setting pay bands. This is not competency-based job evaluation, as the grade structure produced by the original evaluation system is usually left intact. As with the grading system itself, there are various methods for setting pay against grading. These include systems where basic pay is:

- set very precisely against each level/grade – ie every person on the same level/grade will earn the same basic pay
- set as a range between minimum and maximum – ie people on the same level/grade could be on different salaries, but not less than the minimum or more than the maximum
- not set to any limits – ie negotiated with the individual based on what they can contribute to the organisation.

The level of pay agreed against the grading system is likely to change from time to time. Many organisations regularly negotiate new pay levels (often each year). The grading system is, however, unlikely to change unless there is organisational change.

Pay

There are various component parts to 'pay'. These include:

- basic pay
- commission
- bonuses
- profit-sharing
- allowances.

Many of these will be linked either to length of service (eg some bonuses will be awarded only to individuals who have been employed for a certain length of time, regardless of their grade) or directly to the grade or role an individual holds (eg some allowances will be payable only to people in certain job grades). Other elements of pay, however, are linked to the performance of an individual (eg basic pay in performance-related pay schemes or commission). Competency frameworks can contribute where pay is linked to performance.

The main advantage of using competencies as one of the contributions to setting pay bands is that this should help to:

- link the 'how' of job performance to reward
- make job value appear more open
- demonstrate a developmental progression for reward.

Linking job performance to reward

Performance-related pay (PRP) systems, where financial reward is based on performance, are becoming increasingly popular. Some organisations with PRP systems call them competency-based pay. Strictly speaking this is 'competence'-based pay because the competency frameworks include 'output'-based knowledge and skill requirements as well as 'input'-based behavioural competencies. Competency-based pay in its pure form (ie only based on ratings against behavioural indicators) is very unusual and is not advisable because, without clearly defined outputs, there is a danger that nothing gets produced (see the 'Blinkered banking' example on page 127).

There have been many debates about the relevance of linking performance with pay in a direct way. A key point in these debates is whether pay should be to reward people for past performance or to motivate people to perform well in the future, or both. A position that causes less heated debate is that lack of money (as perceived by the job-holder) in relation to input of effort and the type of job being undertaken is perceived to be demotivating. We do not propose a particular view in this debate – but for the purposes of this chapter we will assume that performance does have a bearing on pay, and that organisations who make this link will want to make it as objective as possible.

Most PRP systems require performance to be measured against objectives or targets of some sort, and the outcome of the assessment to be linked to the pay that the individual will receive. The subject of measuring performance has already been covered in depth elsewhere in this book (primarily Chapter 5 – **Using Competencies to Review Performance**). This section looks at how the outcomes of that measurement can be tied in to pay.

The outcomes of performance review and assessment are likely to be in the form of one or more ratings. This may be based on outputs (ie what has been achieved) or inputs (ie how it has been achieved), or a combination of both. In pay systems that measure inputs as well as outputs the final rating is usually a single digit or letter which is arrived at by combining ratings given for both elements.

Whatever rating approach is used, there should be some link between the rating (ie the performance of an individual) and the resulting pay decision. Whether pay is seen as a motivator and/or a reward, everyone in the organisation should be clear about how their performance assessments link in with their pay awards.

The link between performance assessments and pay awards must also tie in with the pay and grading policy. For example, if the policy states that the highest pay awards are to go to those with the highest performance scores, this must be seen to be happening. That, of course, assumes that the pay and grading policy is correct and fair, and is properly implemented too. Discrepancies between the results of PRP awards and the pay policy may be a sign that the policy needs review!

In communicating the pay and grading policy, the competency framework – if it is relevant – should be referred to. As with grading, using competencies to link performance with pay will reinforce the framework's relevance across all the aspects of managing people. This also reinforces the importance that the organisation gives to behaviour in performance. If the people in an organisation have access to the framework, there should be no secrets over how their performance links in with their pay when it comes to competencies.

Mixed messages

An international electronics consumer goods company introduced a competency-based development programme. However, the majority of its staff received pay increases and bonuses based primarily upon targets for the sales of products.

Although some work was under way to link competencies to the pay and grading system, nothing had been done to communicate this work or the perceived importance of competencies to those who would be affected by them.

When individuals received feedback from the development programme regarding their behaviour, they disputed the relevance of the development advice. The messages individuals were taking from pay and grading appeared to be more real and relevant than the messages from the training and development specialists.

Blinkered banking

Several years ago, an international bank began to develop a wholly competency-based pay scheme – on the misguided assumption that if people did things in the right way, they would do the right things in the right way. The scheme was trialled in the United States, but after three years was finally abandoned.

Individuals in the organisation quickly realised that rewards were tied to development and not to activities or output. Some individuals focused as much time as possible on development and were rewarded for doing so – usually at the cost of output from the job. Consequently, development costs rocketed, output dropped, and the pay bill increased.

Pay linked purely to competencies misses the contribution of actual work outputs achieved. For example, if an individual is good at planning, decision-making, teamwork and influencing, but doesn't meet his or her sales targets, an organisation should be questioning what value that individual is bringing to the organisation. The same can be said for just paying on outputs. For example, if an individual exceeds his or her sales targets but does it by working long hours (because he or she is poor at planning) and upsetting everyone he or she meets on the way, then, again, an organisation using a competency framework should question whether it really does value the behaviours endorsed in the framework.

Making job value appear more open
Many job evaluation systems are complex, and in order to understand them and use them effectively, job analysts have to be trained in various techniques. This can often make job analysis a bit of a mystery to most people in the organisation. And, as with many mysteries, folklore builds up. Although it is jobs that are graded, it is people who hold them, and people understand that their pay will be affected by what grade their job is evaluated at. If individuals believe that budgets and the number of people they manage make all the difference between one grade and the next, there is a danger that, come job re-evaluation, there will be considerable emphasis on those features of their jobs. This is perhaps more of an issue in today's flatter organisations where often one of the rare chances of 'promotion' is to get one's job regraded!

The advantage of using a competency-based approach is that the competency framework is available for everyone to see. It can be made quite clear that the competencies in someone's role/job profile are the ones that were not only used to recruit them, but also the ones which contributed to their job grade, and that they will form the framework for some of their performance objectives. Obviously, this still keeps other aspects of the job evaluation system 'hidden', but it is a step in the direction of openness.

Demonstrating a developmental progression for reward
Some organisations will be clear about how a person can progress through certain pay structures to reach a given level of pay. For example, management trainee schemes will often tie progress to pay rises, and some organisations have induction programmes for new job-holders to move them quickly to a 'market rate' for the job.

Competency frameworks allow both job-holders and managers to clearly identify the behaviours that the job-holder needs to display in order to progress along the pay scale – assuming that they also deliver the necessary job outputs. Organisations using this approach are clearly stating that pay is linked not only to what a person produces in the job, but also how they produce it.

Measurement of progress should ideally be done from actual performance in the job. What better way of knowing if someone is demonstrating the required behaviours? We discuss the issue of running assessment for development centres for this type of progress check in Chapter 6 (**Using Competencies for Training and Development**).

Other issues for consideration with pay and grading

There are four other issues we wish to consider regarding pay and grading:

- how over-achievement should be dealt with
- team versus individual pay
- how performance-related pay (PRP) affects personal development
- equal pay.

Rewarding over-achievement

We mentioned in the grading section of this chapter that some organisations overlay their competency framework on their grading structure to help decide on levels of pay. Obviously, each job is likely to require a range of different competencies, and the organisation has to decide which ones should be directly linked with pay.

If achievement of a certain level of competency is rewarded, then the question of over-achievement must be considered. Is the organisation willing to pay more for competency levels achieved over and above those required for a current job? There may be times when this is desirable – when a pool of talent is being nurtured for succession-planning reasons or when a learning culture is being encouraged, for example. However, even when it is desirable, the organisation should make it clear:

- how people can over-achieve
- who is going to rate their performance
- what will happen if over-achievement equals levels of competency that match jobs outside the pay limit for their grade.

There is a balance to be achieved when rewarding over-achievement of competency levels. This is between encouraging people to improve to meet whatever the objective of the policy is, and the danger of raising competency levels beyond that which is required in the short or medium term. There is also the issue of paying people for competencies, or competency levels, that they may never use. This may result in the salary bill being larger than has been budgeted for.

One way of rewarding the achievement of competency is to create the incentive without rewarding it with money. For example, if career progression relies on an individual demonstrating a willingness to achieve levels of competency over and above those that are required for his or her current job, this would not only be an incentive, but would also restrict this achievement to those for whom career development is a motivator.

If monetary reward is considered important, however, an organisation may wish to consider bonus payments. These can be one-off payments for the achievement of competency. They reward achievement without unnecessarily increasing the salary budget over the long term. However, issues such as why people would be motivated to achieve such levels of competency and what the long-term benefit is to the organisation have clearly to be considered before introducing such a scheme.

Team versus individual pay

Many organisations are putting more and more emphasis on teams. The issue of how to reward the people in those teams still seems to be perplexing reward specialists. The key question is still how to motivate and reward individual performance while maintaining an emphasis on the team.

This issue becomes particularly relevant in organisations where a competency framework has been established that focuses on job competency requirements that are, on the whole, expected to be fulfilled by individuals.

Most organisations want to focus on the team because they don't want job-holders to achieve their individual objectives to the detriment of the wider team or organisation. Some also believe that the total is greater than the sum of the parts – in other words, organisational success is often better achieved through teamwork than through the efforts of a number of individuals loosely called a 'team' merely because they report to the same manager.

A competency framework can help balance the objectives of the individual and the team by highlighting team-based behaviour within the framework. The **Appendix Framework** has team-based behaviours included throughout the whole framework. For example, in 'SHOWS THE WAY: Leadership, Level 1' team behaviour is explicit: 'Actively promotes collaboration and teamworking within and across departments' (see page 132). In 'GROWS INDIVIDUAL CAPABILITY: Developing, Level 3' team behaviour is implied: 'Provides support and feedback to colleagues when needed' (see page 134).

An organisation that assesses performance entirely on an individual's output will find it hard to address the issues of behaviour detrimental to the team. Using a competency framework that includes teamworking behaviours allows the importance of teamwork to be demonstrated through all management processes.

Affects of PRP on development
One of the drawbacks of tying performance in so closely with pay is the distraction it causes when discussing less than acceptable performance. Knowing that acknowledging that a competency is not a strength may result in an erosion of a pay rise may lead to people playing down the issue or avoiding it altogether. It is also a distraction for the manager, who may not want to demotivate a staff member in this way.

The issue can be tackled by setting learning objectives. This may be particularly relevant for trainees in the job who can't be expected to achieve the same level of output or competency as their more experienced peers. A learning objective will focus on the achievement of certain levels of competency or output within certain time-frames and with agreed support. Assuming that the trainee is already being paid at the lower end of the pay range, he or she can still achieve acceptable performance ratings while discussing development and progress. The setting of learning objectives is covered in Chapter 6 (**Using Competencies for Training and Development**).

Another way of tackling this issue is to split the discussion about achievement of objectives away from the discussion about development needs. If objectives are clearly established, measurement of performance against them should be relatively easy. The output from this discussion can then feed into pay. Another discussion, held at a completely different time and following a different cycle, can then be held on the subject of training and development needs.

As long as pay and performance are closely linked, this issue will never be completely resolved. However, there are ways to minimise the distraction of pay when discussing performance, and organisations should think through carefully how they are going to tackle the issue.

Equal pay
The Equal Pay Act 1970 states that a person of one sex must not be treated less favourably than a person of the opposite sex who works for the same employer, as regards pay and other terms of the contract of employment, where they are employed on:

- like work
- work that has been rated as equivalent under a job evaluation scheme
- work that is of equal value.

We mention equal pay here for two reasons. Firstly, if an organisation is using their competency framework to link pay to grading, they must be absolutely certain that they are not building inequalities into the process via the design of the framework. In Chapter 2 (**A Typical Competency Framework**) we mention that a quality framework will be fair to all employees. When developing the framework, it is important to consider all potential sources of bias. To reiterate the example used in Chapter 2, a management competency framework compiled using data collected only from older, white, male managers may not be fair to everyone, because it may exclude behaviours that could be observed in effective managers who do not come from this sample.

Secondly, competencies can be used to help design pay systems that are fair to all. Outlining some of the pitfalls in current pay systems that can lead to equal pay issues, Allison, Brett and Hatchett (2002) included the following:

> - 'broadbanded pay structures that mean widely differing salaries can be paid for the same job
> - incremental pay scales that reward long service over relevant experience
> - a lack of progression or a structured process to reach a rate for the job
> - performance pay systems that allow human judgement to lead to discrimination in pay
> - job evaluation schemes that place more weight on "hard" skills such as physical effort or formal qualifications and undervalue caring factors or responsibility for people.'

Well-designed competency frameworks can help to eliminate unfairness in each of the above issues. Used in job evaluation they can provide a structure within which 'soft', behavioural issues can be described. They will also be invaluable when it comes to managing the people within those jobs. Well-defined competencies and management processes will help managers to identify what 'relevant experience' and 'caring' look like, for example, and will help remove much of the subjective judgement associated with less well-structured performance appraisal systems. The use of competencies in development and performance appraisal are covered elsewhere in this book.

Competency frameworks will not replace 'hard' skills in evaluation systems, but used alongside them they can help make the systems fairer and more effective.

KEY POINTS

- Competency-related pay is becoming less popular. However, the use of competencies in performance management is increasing. As performance is often linked to pay, either directly or indirectly, competencies and pay continue to be a relevant topic for many managers.
- The close link between grading structures and the pay that is attached to the jobs that fall within that structure make pay and grading difficult to separate. However, they both attempt to apply relative values of a job or an individual to the organisation.

- The value of a job or role is indicated by its relative position in the hierarchy of the grading systems.

- The contribution that competencies make to job evaluation is in providing additional information to create a more rounded picture of a job. If competencies are used in other people-management activities, the message is that these behaviours are valued. If job evaluation is about measuring the elements of a job which an organisation values, it makes sense to include competencies in that process.

- The value of individuals is indicated by the job or role they are doing, how they are doing it, and the rewards they receive.

- Pay is the financial reward that individuals receive for the work they do.

- Performance-related pay (PRP) links the level of financial reward that an individual receives to his or her performance in the job. Although this is often called 'competency-based pay', it is actually 'competence-based pay', because the frameworks used include 'output'-based knowledge and skill requirements as well as 'input' -based behavioural competencies.

- Competency-based pay is where pay is linked to competency ratings alone. Very few organisations use competencies alone to evaluate jobs and create grading structures.

- Concentration on payment just for results (outputs) misses the important aspect of *how* a job is performed. Payment just for the display of competency misses the importance of producing results.

- How organisations will deal with over-achievement in relation to reward must be considered. If it is to be encouraged (eg for succession planning or to support a learning culture), organisations must consider how it will be rewarded. Non-financial rewards can be used to keep down the salary budget but still provide an incentive.

- Many organisations wish to encourage teamwork whilst setting individual objectives. Competencies describing teamworking behaviours can be used to address this potential conflict when it comes to reward.

- If development needs are seen as detrimental to pay rises, they may not be addressed effectively if they are discussed at the same time as an individual's pay-related performance. For many, it may be more beneficial to split development discussions from performance for pay reviews.

- Competencies can assist organisations when it comes to issues of equal pay. They provide a framework to describe the 'soft' elements of a job to ensure that they are appropriately taken into account when assessing the value of a job.

- Pay and grading are complex issues, and there are no clear answers or one 'right' way of tackling them. The key role that competencies can play in these processes is to improve the completeness of information being used to grade jobs and allocate pay. Competencies are therefore a factor in the process, not the process itself. Organisations that take an integrative approach to their competency framework need to ensure that the value they are placing on behaviours is endorsed through all of their people-management processes – including pay and grading.

REFERENCES AND READING

ALLISON N., BRETT S. and HATCHETT A. (2002) 'A square deal'. *People Management*. Vol. 8, No. 14, 11 July. pp14–15.

RANKIN N. (2002) 'Benchmarking Survey'. *Competency & Emotional Intelligence*. (Benchmarking edition). pp13.

Sample competency framework

CLUSTER 1: SHOWS THE WAY

DIRECTION: Uses accurate business knowledge to achieve common goals

Level 1 Develops strategies that account for the short-, medium- and long-term needs of the business

- Produces and regularly communicates three-to-five-year plans to ensure strategies remain relevant
- Balances long-term goals with short-term deliverables to achieve business goals
- Ensures business goals are communicated and understood across the business.

Level 2 Keeps others informed of business goals and inspires buy-in to them

- Develops local goals to support wider business goals
- Inspires buy-in to business goals by showing how individual efforts contribute to them
- Provides timely and appropriate information to support achievement of business goals.

Level 3 Supports business goals by addressing issues likely to affect achieving them

- Focuses and encourages others to focus on delivering the business goals
- Regularly reviews and communicates progress on business goals
- Uses the business goals to prioritise work.

LEADERSHIP: Provides clear leadership consistent with our vision, mission and values

Level 1 Is consistent in expectations of others and provides clear leadership

- Provides a role model for managers through use of the competency behaviours and business values
- Exudes energy and enthusiasm for achieving business goals with a 'can-do, will-do' approach
- Actively promotes collaboration and teamworking within and across departments.

Level 2 Operates openly, is accessible and approachable to others

- Communicates openly and honestly
- Ensures the impact of their own behaviour on others is positive
- Accepts responsibility for decisions and actions, including difficult but necessary ones.

PLANNING: Sets and agrees plans for self and/or others based on business goals

Level 1 Ensures business plans are achievable and integrated with business goals

- Develops and communicates performance measures for business plans
- Allocates appropriate resources to enable business plans to be executed.

Level 2 Ensures plans meet local needs and that they account for the needs of other teams

- Highlights key milestones and celebrates success in reaching them
- Works within and across business functions to plan and achieve objectives
- Ensures plans are compatible with wider business goals.

Level 3 Uses appropriate planning to succeed in own role

- Sets SMART objectives for self and/or team
- Regularly reviews progress of plans to redirect action when necessary
- Considers 'what ifs' and uses contingency plans to minimise risks
- Plans activities based on the needs of those who will be affected by them.

CLUSTER 2: GROWS BUSINESS CAPABILITY

IMPROVEMENT FOCUS: Encourages and generates ideas to enhance future business performance

Level 1 Promotes a business-wide culture of continuous improvement

- Seeks and promotes innovation to take the business forward
- Works to establish an environment where individuals feel opinions and ideas are welcomed.

Level 2 Facilitates improvements within teams and across departments

- Quickly translates ideas with potential business benefits into actions
- Champions change when it is required
- Encourages the sharing of experiences to improve performance.

Level 3 Contributes and encourages others to contribute to new ideas

- Responds positively to challenges from others
- Offers new ideas and solutions to current challenges
- Tests new ideas with others
- Readily adopts new ways of working.

BUSINESS FOCUS: Uses understanding of the business to improve results

Level 1 Uses industry knowledge to enhance overall business performance

- Monitors external environment to minimise its negative impact on business results
- Ensures efficient cross-business working to minimise wasted effort
- Uses knowledge of the external environment to maximise opportunities for the business.

Level 2 Manages competing business needs to deliver improved results

- Manages the introduction of new initiatives with minimum disruption to pursuit of business goals
- Regularly reviews activities, events and projects to ensure they contribute to business goals
- Uses strategic alliances to enhance achievement of business results.

Level 3 Ensures own role continues to add value to the business

- Focuses personal effort on activities that contribute to business performance
- Seeks relevant advice/information from appropriate sources
- Ensures role relationships with customers and/or suppliers add value.

CUSTOMER FOCUS: Uses understanding of the needs of customers to drive action

Level 1 Champions customer focus throughout the business

- Ensures others understand the importance of the customer both now and in the future
- Actively considers the customer when creating or reviewing initiatives
- Anticipates the future needs of customers and builds these into plans.

Level 2 Actively manages worthwhile relationships with customers

- Seeks feedback from customers to enhance services and/or products
- Responds appropriately to customer requests
- Establishes customer information needs in order to communicate effectively with customers.

CLUSTER 3: GROWS INDIVIDUAL CAPABILITY

DEVELOPING: Demonstrates trust and confidence in the ability of others

Level 1 Ensures development is treated as a priority for business success

- Empowers people to make appropriate decisions at all levels
- Personally champions the importance of training, development and succession planning across the business
- Displays confidence in all levels of management by showing appropriate trust in their ability to do their job.

Level 2 Takes action to ensure individuals can fulfil the demands of their roles

- Develops accountability and responsibility in their team
- Ensures people know the scope of their roles
- Promotes understanding of their department across the company.

Level 3 Supports the achievement of role demands

- Provides support and feedback to colleagues when needed
- Helps people to learn from mistakes
- Identifies and removes or works around blocks to progress, as appropriate.

MANAGING PERFORMANCE: Inspires ownership and achievement of standards

Level 1 Ensures performance management is effective across the business

- Balances the management of people and initiatives across the business
- Takes account of the needs of own and others' departments when setting objectives
- Uses best practice benchmarks to monitor performance of departments.

Level 2 Provides effective management support for their department

- Effectively balances management of people, tasks and activities
- Encourages others to have a realistic view of their career prospects
- Takes account of the needs of team members when agreeing objectives

Level 3 Manages day-to-day performance constructively, fairly and promptly

- Openly recognises and rewards good performance
- Acts quickly and fairly to address poor performance
- Demonstrates the importance of performance management by giving it a high priority
- Is open to and encourages feedback from all levels in the business
- Visibly and quickly deals with those who harass, bully or unfairly discriminate.

Checklist: Qualities of a good competency framework

QUALITIES OF A GOOD COMPETENCY FRAMEWORK		
Assess your framework using the following questions. Before answering a question, think about how you know the answer to be true – if necessary, consult or test your views with designers and users of the framework.		
Address any area where the answer is 'no'. Chapter 3 contains information on how to design and/or update a competency framework.		
	Yes	No
Is the framework clear and easy to understand?		
1. Is the language unambiguous, simple and straightforward?		
2. Is the structure of the framework as simple as it could be?		
3. Is the framework structured logically?		
Is the framework relevant to all those who will be affected by it?		
4. Are users able to relate the competency headings and definitions to their jobs?		
5. If appropriate, are users able to relate the competency-level definitions to their jobs?		
6. Are users able to relate the behaviours to their jobs?		
Does the framework take account of expected changes?		
7. Will the framework still apply when planned organisational restructuring takes place?		
8. Have planned changes in technology been taken into account?		
9. Has the framework been designed to cater for expected changes in organisational culture and/or values?		
10. Does the framework take account of expected changes in the organisation's operating environment?		

	Yes	No
Does the framework have discrete elements?		
11. Do competencies only appear in one place in the framework?		
12. Do behavioural indicators only appear in one place in the framework?		
13. Are all the behaviours necessary for effective performance in the jobs for which the framework was designed?		
14. Do individual behaviours describe single examples of competency?		
15. Do the behaviours describe observable examples of competency?		
16. Does each behaviour contain an 'action'?		
17. Does each behaviour contain enough contextual information to describe why the action is necessary?		
Are elements of the same type?		
18. Do the behavioural indicators describe behaviours rather than personal characteristics such as knowledge, technical skills and abilities?		
19. Do the competency headings and definitions summarise actions and contexts rather than skills or knowledge?		
Are behaviours necessary and appropriate?		
20. Are behaviours based on good procedures and safe practices?		
21. Will the behaviours help to enhance and/or ensure effective performance?		
Has the framework been designed to be as fair as possible to all users?		
22. Is the framework based on data collected from a wide range of people (different ages, ethnic backgrounds, gender, etc)?		
23. Does the framework include indicators of effective, but perhaps not normally witnessed, behaviours?		

Producing competency-based role profiles

Most competency applications will require information about the relevance of specific competencies or competency levels to specific jobs. One way of developing and recording this information is by producing a competency-based role profile. The following guidelines are just that – guidelines. In practice, the process outlined below will need to be adapted and facilitated by someone experienced in this type of activity.

Step 1 – Job purpose – Competency-based role profiles start with clarifying the job purpose. This is a brief statement of the contribution that the job makes to the department or organisation. For example:

- Develop and manage a client portfolio for yourself and the team.
- Deliver a profit income of £500,000.
- Maintain a team capable of delivering current year targets.
- Develop self and the team in order to increase profit capability by 12% per year.

Step 2 – Key activities – Having identified the job purpose, the next step is to identify the key activities that must be performed effectively in order that the job purpose can be fulfilled. Typically these will be eight to ten in number, and contain activities such as managing team performance, project planning, co-ordinating team resources and so on.

Step 3 – Competency weightings – Key activities are then used to produce weightings for the importance of competencies or competency levels for the role. The following type of grid can be used for this. A rating system is used to enter scores into the grid – a tick system has been used in this example to indicate how critical each competency level is for each key activity.

A total score is then calculated for each competency level. In this example the number of ticks in each column have simply been added together. In practice a more sophisticted system of rating and scoring is likely to be used – such as a rating scale with three or four scale-points, each with detailed scale definitions, and possibly a weighted scoring system to accommodate key activities with differing degrees of importance.

Key activities	Competency levels (competency.level)											
	1.1	1.2	1.3	2.1	2.2	2.3	3.1	3.2	3.3	4.1	4.2	etc
1	✓✓	✓		✓✓	✓✓					✓		
2		✓✓					✓✓	✓✓	✓✓	✓		
3		✓✓			✓		✓✓	✓✓		✓	✓	
etc												
Total	2	5	–	2	3	–	4	4	2	3	1	

Key: ✓ – some behaviours are critical to this activity
        ✓✓ – all behaviours are critical to this activity
        blank – no behaviours are critical to this activity

In most cases the level of competency with the highest total score is likely to be the level required for the profile. So for this example (where the higher the level number, the higher the competency level) the competency-based role profile would be competency 1 level 2; competency 2 level 2; competency 3 level 2; competency 4 level 1 and so on.

In some instances it may be that a key activity is so central to the role that all levels of competency receive the highest rating. In this case, the highest level of competency that received a critical rating would be recorded in the role profile. In this example, lets assume this is the case for key activity 2, in which case competency 3 level 3 would be entered on the profile.

Role profiles are ideally compiled as and when needed by job-holders and their managers under the initial guidance of a facilitator. Each individual prepares their view of job purpose and key activities. These are then agreed before completing the grid.

To ensure that competency-based role profiles are current, we recommend that they are produced only when needed. Where a generic, organisation-wide competency framework exists, the process for producing role profiles, and what they should look like when they are produced, should be the same throughout the organisation. This ensures that the benefits of a generic competency framework (eg encouraging comparisons between roles for development purposes) are not lost. A consistent process and output will also enable the organisation to hold central records of profiles (preferably on an easily updated computer system, available to all employees).

To ensure that roles can be quickly profiled when needed, it is advisable to disseminate the necessary skills required among key individuals, especially within large organisations. These key individuals may be local HR managers/advisers and/or line managers who are experienced in people management. Where such local arrangements are made, it is important that standards and consistency are monitored and maintained through a central co-ordinating function, such as the HR department. This is particularly important where competency-based role profiles affect such organisation-wide issues as pay, grading and progression.

Index